T0340364

"This inspiring book points the way to a new kind of governance: collaborative, problem-solving, creative, and long-term oriented. Climate change is a complex crisis requiring deep and sustained changes across society—in how we produce and use energy, protect nature, adapt to environmental stresses, and ensure social justice. As described in the inspiring case studies, stakeholders across society are joining together to chart the way ahead. This book gives hope, guidance, and direction for the future."

Jeffrey D. Sachs, Director, Center for Sustainable Development,
Columbia University; President, United Nations Sustainable
Development Solutions Network; author of The Age of
Sustainable Development

"This book will be a must read for anyone working on climate resilience, providing critical insights into how to achieve our climate goals and preserve our communities, using collaboration and partnerships as key tools. Through practical case studies, the authors take the reader into key communities, from New York City to the West Point Military Academy, that are tackling their climate challenges, through collaboration, shared decision-making, and smart use of big data."

Sherri Goodman, former Deputy Undersecretary of Defense
(Environmental Security), Secretary-General, International
Military Council on Climate & Security

"As I've observed over and over again in my career working with diverse entities—government, companies, nonprofit organizations—it can be a daunting task to resolve differences on a clean economy in the face of climate change. This book offers superb examples of real-life parties who accomplished this essential feat to save the planet."

Jigar Shah, Founder of SunEdison, co-founder of Generate
Capital, author of Creating Climate Wealth

"This book comes at a moment of consensus among advocates that there will not be effective climate policies until diverse stakeholders seek alignment on climate issues where they can, and also acknowledge their conflicting views and remedies. Collaboration is the watchword and Mesa and Goodman offer a guide to how untraditional partners have convened to achieve beneficial climate objectives."

Peggy M. Shepard, executive director, co-founder,
WE ACT for Environmental Justice

"Climate change has been politically divisive at the national level, but solving this existential threat will require cooperation across multiple sectors of society at every level. This book by two experienced practitioners skillfully recounts remarkable examples where this cooperation has been achieved to the benefit of all. It will be an inspiration and a toolkit for those who are yearning for solutions."

Michael Gerrard, *Professor and Director, Sabin Center for Climate Change Law, Columbia University*

"Planning for resilience in the face of climate change requires planners to simultaneously work across disciplines and at multiple layers of community, city, and region. It challenges planners to respond in new ways and collaborate outside traditional formulas. This book shows, through case studies of both public and private initiatives, how we can achieve better outcomes and face up to this generational threat. Their lessons have broad applications, and should be incorporated in every plan to create more resilient communities."

Tom Wright, *President, Regional Plan Association*

"The only possible path for successfully stopping the impending catastrophe of climate change is through a coordinated and united effort that includes institutions from local governments and businesses to organizations that have the power to influence global policy. Ann Goodman and Nilda Mesa's new volume, *Collaborating for Climate Resilience*, expertly details the kind of reality-based collaborative approaches that marshal the science, resources and human will that are our best hope for meeting this still neglected challenge."

David Rosenberg, *Professor and Director, Zicklin Center for Corporate Integrity, Zicklin School of Business, Baruch College, City University of New York (CUNY)*

"The war against climate change will be fought on many fronts by armies of stakeholders drawn from all sectors of society as this book illustrates in providing examples of successful victories built on collaboration and cooperation among a range of public and private sector players from local to national levels—it's a must read for the decade to come."

Eugenie L. Birch *FAICP, Nussdorf Professor and co-Director, Penn Institute for Urban Research, University of Pennsylvania*

"At this moment of deep political division and mistrust, Nilda Mesa and Ann Goodman provide a different and hopeful path: cooperation and collaboration as the essential route to community resilience in the face of climate change. Mesa and Goodman provide a handbook for everyone who cares about the way forward."

Ken Alex, *Director, Project Climate at UC Berkeley's Center for Law, Energy & Environment, former senior policy advisor to California Governor Jerry Brown*

"The sense of urgency and scale of the climate crisis can be paralyzing, especially in light of the impacts from the pandemic. This timely book helps clarify how we can all work collaboratively to make the transformation toward climate resilience that is urgently needed. The authors have assembled climate resilience case studies demonstrating the power of collaboration in a wide variety of scales, multiple perspectives and topics. The common lessons learned of seeking aligned values, collaboration, adaptability, and accountability will resonate for anyone committed to a climate-resilient future."

Mary Ann Lazarus, FAIA LEED Fellow, Architect and Consultant, Cameron MacAllister Group Sustainability Program Coordinator, University College, Washington University in St. Louis

"Every urban planner in America should read this book."

Maxine Griffith, College of Fellows—American Institute of Certified Planners, Principal, Griffith Planning and Design, former Assistant Deputy Secretary US Department of Housing and Urban Affairs, former Executive Director, Philadelphia City Planning Commission and Deputy Mayor

"Mesa and Goodman do an amazing job of spotlighting the evolution of state and local government, not-for-profits and business to identify and implement climate solutions that provide both economic and social benefit at the local level, which have positive implications at the global level."

Ann Davlin, Director of Strategy, Dynamhex, former Director of Development, Carbon War Room

"There is extraordinary value in gathering emerging models and recognizing new systems that are critical in achieving long-term climate adaptation. This publication, Collaborating for Climate Resilience, assembles those emerging models as artifacts, proven structures, for further examination and potential replicating across the globe. Collaboration is key to creating a sustainable resilient future."

Illya Azaroff, FAIA, Global Director, Resilient Strategies, +LAB Architect PLLC., Founding Co-chair, Design for Risk and Reconstruction, AIA New York, Associate Professor, New York City College of Technology

"Libraries are filled with books addressing the question of 'what' to do to improve climate resilience. Rarer are books that tell us 'how'. Nilda Mesa and Ann Goodman's Collaborating for Climate Resilience fills that critical void. Through organizational case studies they show us how government, business and civil society have effectively collaborated to address this urgent global challenge."

Elliott Sclar, Special Research Scholar & Co-Director, Center for Sustainable Urban Development, Earth Institute, Professor Emeritus of Urban Planning, Graduate School of Architecture, Planning and Preservation, Columbia University

"*Collaborating for Climate Resilience* takes on an aspect of the climate problem that doesn't generate many headlines, but that is absolutely critical: how diverse organizations can effectively work together to adapt. It compiles case studies from state and local government, the military, and the private sector, analyzes both successes and failures, and draws instructive lessons for future climate leaders."

Adam Sobel, *Professor, Applied Physics and Applied Mathematics and Lamont-Doherty Earth Observatory, Columbia University*

Collaborating for Climate Resilience

Supporters of environmental well-being and climate resilience are awakening and mobilizing – cities, states, business, academia, community-based organizations, and the military. They understand the imminent and long-term risks of climate deterioration and they are creating new structures beyond the top-down government policy efforts of the past.

This highly practical book provides a clear insight into these collaborative solutions by real organizations in real time. It demonstrates how people from disparate fields and stakeholders cooperate to address climate issues at ground level and reveals how this can be undertaken effectively. Through case studies of key organizations such as the NYC Sustainability Office, Detroiters Working for Environmental Justice, IBM, and West Point Military Academy, readers will understand each party's role in a cooperative enterprise and the means by which they support climate resiliency, their institutional goals, and their communities.

Of particular value, the book illustrates the co-benefits of multi-party resilience planning: faster approval times; reduced litigation; ability to monetize benefits such as positive health outcomes; the economic benefits of cooperation (for example, capacity building through financing climate planning and resilience across public, private, and other sources of funding); and developing a shared perspective. The book will be of great interest to business managers, policymakers, and community leaders involved in combating climate change, and researchers and students of business, public affairs, policy, environment, climate, and urban studies.

Ann Goodman, PhD, is Faculty Affiliate in the Graduate Center, City University of New York (CUNY), Advanced Science Research Center (ASRC), Environmental Sciences Initiative, with 30 years of international leadership at the intersection of business, finance, sustainability, climate, risk, resilience, as for- and nonprofit executive, entrepreneur, communicator, author, and educator.

Nilda Mesa is Visiting Lecturer at the Paris School of International Affairs, SciencesPo, and Adjunct Professor at the School of International and Public Affairs, Columbia University. She serves on the Board of Directors of United Therapeutics. Mesa is the former director of the New York City Mayor's Office of Sustainability, and served in senior environmental roles at the US Environmental Protection Agency, the Pentagon, and the White House Council on Environmental Quality.

Giving Voice to Values
Series Editor: Mary C. Gentile

The *Giving Voice to Values* series is a collection of books on Business Ethics and Corporate Social Responsibility that brings a practical, solutions-oriented, skill-building approach to the salient questions of values-driven leadership.

Giving Voice to Values (GVV: www.GivingVoiceToValues.org) – the curriculum, the pedagogy and the research upon which it is based – was designed to transform the foundational assumptions upon which the teaching of business ethics is based, and importantly, to equip future business leaders to know not only what is right – but how to make it happen.

Collaborating for Climate Resilience

Ann Goodman and Nilda Mesa

Routledge
Taylor & Francis Group

LONDON AND NEW YORK

First published 2022
by Routledge
2 Park Square, Milton Park, Abingdon, Oxon OX14 4RN

and by Routledge
605 Third Avenue, New York, NY 10158

Routledge is an imprint of the Taylor & Francis Group, an informa business

British Library Cataloguing-in-Publication Data
A catalogue record for this book is available from the British Library

Library of Congress Cataloging-in-Publication Data
A catalog record has been requested for this book

ISBN: 978-0-367-23709-7 (hbk)
ISBN: 978-0-367-23705-9 (pbk)
ISBN: 978-0-429-28124-2 (ebk)

DOI: 10.4324/9780429281242

Typeset in Bembo
by Newgen Publishing UK

Contents

Contributors

Elizabeth Andrews is the director of William & Mary Law School's Virginia Coastal Policy Center. She formerly served as senior assistant attorney general and chief of the Environmental section, Virginia Office of the Attorney General, where she oversaw a team of attorneys representing the state's natural resources agencies. She also served as the water policy manager for the Virginia Department of Environmental Quality, working with the legislature, regulated community, and environmental organizations to address Virginia's water quality and water quantity challenges. She graduated from the College of William & Mary and received her JD degree, *summa cum laude*, from the Washington College of Law, American University.

Tanya Denckla Cobb is Director of the Institute for Engagement & Negotiation (IEN) at the University of Virginia. At IEN since 1997, she is a public policy mediator with experience in a broad range of issues and processes that support resilient communities and a healthy environment in the context of social equity. A graduate of Smith College, she has led two urban forestry nonprofits, authored two books, and worked for the federal government in international labor rights. In recent years, she has worked on coastal resilience, tobacco harm reduction, environmental justice, contested public spaces and legacies of harm, and food system and food justice issues.

Michelle Covi is an assistant professor of practice at Old Dominion University in the Department of Ocean, Earth, and Atmospheric Sciences and a Virginia Sea Grant extension partner. She conducts research and university-based outreach activities for climate adaptation and coastal resilience for Virginia. Her research areas include sea level rise, resilience risk perception and communication, public participation in adaptation planning processes, and engagement/outreach methodologies. She has a PhD in coastal resources management from East Carolina University and a master's degree in marine science from the University of Georgia, where she studied salt marsh ecology.

Diana Dierks leads global programs covering environmental and social responsibility in IBM's supply chain. Her passion for environmental sustainability and positive impact led her to shift her technical program-management career into supply chain sustainability. She is motivated by the improvements gained when organizations take responsibility for their supply chains as extensions of their core business operations and is proud of IBM's long standing leadership in this space. Prior to her present work, she drove process improvement and automation in IBM's Software as a Service businesses; she has a background in client account executive roles and project management. She holds a BS in computer science from Texas A&M University and is an alumna of IBM's Corporate Service Corps, a corporate citizenship and leader development program that selects and deploys top talent within IBM on a global assignment to help solve societal challenges in emerging markets. In her assignment, she worked with an NGO based in the Philippines, applying rice science to reduce poverty and hunger and ensure the environmental sustainability of rice farming.

Louis Ferretti is the project executive for developing and leading a host of risk and compliance programs across IBM's global-supplier network for environmental compliance, supply chain social responsibility, conflict minerals, sustainability, risk, business continuity, General Data Protection Regulation, and IT/security. He has been a regular speaker at suppy chain industry forums and universities on procurement transformation, suppy chain sustainability, environmental compliance, and risk management. He is a graduate of the City University of New York with a BS in engineering science. He serves on the boards of the Triangle Chapter (Raleigh, NC) of the Institute for Supply Management and the Global Supply Chain Resiliency Council. He is a member of the Arizona State Supply Chain Advisory Board and the UC San Diego Institute for Supply Excellence and Innovation Outreach program.

Ann Goodman, author of *Adapting to Change: The Business of Climate Resilience* (BEP, 2016), is a faculty affiliate at the Graduate Center of City University of New York's Advanced Science Research Center's Environmental Sciences. She has 30 years of international experience in the fields of business, sustainability, climate, risk assessment, and strategic resilience planning as an executive, entrepreneur, communicator, researcher, and educator. She has advised the National Institute of Standards and Technology on the Economics and Society committee and worked with the National Climate Assessment and Development Advisory Committee. She speaks widely on sustainability, climate, and business to international audiences in Europe, Asia, and the Americas; recently throughout the US and in China, Hong Kong, Thailand, France, and Colombia. Earlier in her career, she cofounded the Women's Network for a Sustainable Future and was its executive director. A former full-time journalist, she reported extensively on sustainability/business for *Fortune*, *Business Week*, and Public Radio's *Marketplace*; she was an editor-in-chief at United Newspapers and the first business journalist elected to the

Board of the Society of Environmental Journalists. She has a BA, MA, and a PhD from the University of Chicago; was awarded a French Government Doctoral Research Fellowship; served on the University of Paris business/economics faculty (Dauphine) for five years; and taught at New York University, Bard College, and CUNY's Zicklin School of Business at Baruch College.

Angela M. King is the assistant director of the Virginia Coastal Policy Center (VCPC) at William & Mary Law School. Before joining VCPC, she was an assistant attorney general in the Consumer Protection section of the Virginia Office of the Attorney General, where she focused on charitable solicitation matters. Her professional experience also includes serving as the executive director of the Newport News Green Foundation and as an assistant county attorney for James City County. She received her JD, *magna cum laude*, from Indiana University, Bloomington, and her BS in geography and anthropology, *cum laude*, from Florida State University.

Kimberly Hill Knott spent more than a decade working for former Congressman John Conyers. She then furthered her interest in the political arena by joining the staff of Detroiters Working for Environmental Justice (DWEJ) as policy director. While on staff at DWEJ, she spearheaded the Detroit Climate Action Collaborative, which developed the first Detroit Climate Action Plan, released in 2017. In 2013, she was selected for the White House Champions of Change Award for her work in addressing climate change in Detroit. Currently, she is Chair of the Detroit Green Task Force Climate Action Committee and is President/CEO of Future Insight Consulting, LLC, a firm specializing in corporate sustainability and coalition building around climate change.

Nilda Mesa's career in environment and sustainability spans more than 30 years at the federal, state, and local level, as well as in universities and internationally. She served as director of the New York City Mayor's Office of Sustainability, directing and principal author and editor of OneNYC (2015), the city's innovative long-term sustainability plan, and founded Columbia University's sustainability office, winning awards in both positions. Previously, she served in senior advisory positions with the White House Council on Environmental Quality, the Pentagon, and the US Environmental Protection Agency, as counsel to the US North American Free Trade Agreement (NAFTA) Task Force on the environmental side agreements. As a deputy attorney general in the environment section of the California Attorney General's office, she worked on environmental justice litigation. She has extensive international experience. Currently, she is Director of the Urban Sustainability and Equity Planning Program of the Center for Sustainable Urban Development in the Earth Institute and Adjunct Professor at Columbia University's School of International and Public Affairs, as well as a visiting professor at the Paris School of International Affairs at Sciences Po and a visiting scholar at its Laboratory for Interdisciplinary Evaluation of Public Policies. She writes, speaks, and teaches about climate, energy, equity, and sustainability planning and content at the urban and global scale, incorporating design and creative techniques with policy planning and research on urban systems, public health, and economic inclusion. She is a member of the board of directors of United Therapeutics. She is a graduate of Harvard Law School and Northwestern University.

Mark R. Read was commissioned a second lieutenant in the US Army Infantry upon graduation from the US Military Academy (USMA), West Point, in 1992 with a BS in Environmental Engineering. He holds an MS and PhD in geography from Pennsylvania State University. During his 27 years in the Army, he has served in a variety of assignments and locations throughout the United States and overseas, including Germany, Bosnia-Herzegovina, Kuwait, and Iraq. He currently holds the rank of Colonel, and serves as a professor at USMA and Head of the Department of Geography and Environmental Engineering at West Point. His academic interests include climate variability and change, environmental security, and military geography.

Augusta C.F. Wilson is an attorney at the Climate Science Legal Defense Fund (CSLDF). Before joining CSLDF, she held a fellowship at NYU Law School's Guarini Center for Environmental, Energy, and Land Use Law. Chapter 6 is based in part on research she conducted while at the Guarini Center and published in the *Columbia Journal of Environmental Law*. Prior to her fellowship, she was an attorney with the Clean Air Council in Philadelphia. She received her JD from Cornell Law School and a BA in biochemistry from Case Western Reserve University.

Foreword

This "foreword" might more accurately be labeled an "afterthought." It follows many months of global lockdown due to a world health crisis—namely, the COVID-19 pandemic—along with a US national political battle, resulting in the election of a new US president, all during an ongoing global climate crisis, with its own health implications, that has taken on political overtones.

This book nonetheless looks to the future. It collects lessons from successful collaborations that overcame conflicts of policy, economic and social priorities among federal, state, and local governments and in the private and nonprofit sectors. These lessons are especially timely now, providing a guide based on real-life cases demonstrating how climate collaborations—often undertaken among widely divergent parties—can be built to succeed for all.

In the efforts recounted throughout these pages, we see successes in rising above the rhetoric to find shared values and approaches to advance common goals, such as clean air, jobs and a strong local economy, resilience in the face of increased natural threats, and community and individual health and well-being. In the pages that follow, collaborating to address climate resilience, the subject of this book, is shown to be not just possible, but the only way to bring to life real climate resilience.

This is not the first time that health concerns have awakened citizens of the world in general, and Americans in particular, to environmental degradation. The groundbreaking 1962 book *Silent Spring* by Rachel Carson, notably a US federal government employee, is widely viewed as launching the US environmental movement, connecting human and wider environmental well-being by focusing on the harm of DDT and pesticides generally.

During 2020, the world found itself again confronting twin crises of human health: namely the COVID-19 coronavirus and climate change. While they may not be directly related, according to experts on biology and public health, both crises can be linked to human excesses, which have harmed the air, water, soil, biodiversity, and other aspects of nature on which all life forms depend. Like so many environmental issues, these are system-wide problems, not necessarily linked to any one activity or single source.

"I am not aware of direct connections between Covid and climate change," said Dr. Samuel S. Myers, principal research scientist, Department of Environmental Health, and director, Planetary Health Alliance, Harvard T.H. Chan School of Public Health. However, he explained:

> What they both share, is a common root in the scale of human disruption of Earth's natural systems. These disruptions are not limited to the climate system but also include global biodiversity loss, land use change, pollution of air, water, and soil, resource scarcity, etc. Our broken relationship with nature helped drive Covid and is also driving climate change.
>
> (personal communication, October 1, 2020)

The need for science-based policymaking, along with collaboration among multiple parties, is especially keen now. A political shift toward a more positive approach that values the environment in general and climate in particular, as well as human health, is likely in the US after the 2020 election of a new president, Joe Biden, who underscores the need for science in his talks and has unveiled proposals for dealing with both human health and climate change.

Indeed, we have been enduring policy transitions for several years, notably since the 2015 COP21 Paris Agreement, which the US initially agreed to and then backed out of under the subsequent US presidency. Yet the climate policy vacuum served to spur increased action by new, powerful players, including leading companies in the private sector and local, state, and regional governments, which see the need to address climate change now.

Local action has proven to be a highly catalyzing and stabilizing force on climate: with the abdication of federal participation, local players have risen to meet the challenge. This vital role is likely to continue, demonstrating key lessons, notably the importance of broad inclusion of stakeholders—from the private and nonprofit sectors, to government, to labor, to community residents—and of wider environmental justice issues.

Moreover, as markets, along with the economy generally, respond to climate challenges, we have seen declining prices for renewable energy, at times becoming cheaper than fossil fuel derived energy sources such as coal. At the same time, budgets in the public and private sectors alike have been slashed due to the economic effects of the COVID-19 pandemic, which has driven widespread unemployment, bankruptcy, and general economic stress. This combination of critical factors shines a glaring light on the urgent need for collaboration among all parties, along with science-based policymaking.

With the 2020 US presidential election, the federal role can be anticipated to evolve again, likely in a more positive direction for the environment generally and climate more specifically, promising to reinstate the US in the Paris Climate Agreement. The growing commitments of local, regional, and private sector efforts over the last four years, and the re-entrance of the US into the

Paris Climate Agreement, bode well for larger international efforts to produce lasting climate solutions.

The lessons in these chapters are more pertinent than ever during our ongoing global climate crisis. In trying times, they offer hope as well as proven techniques for successfully achieving climate resilience.

Acknowledgments

Many individuals and organizations have offered their time and insight to this book, including our essential chapter contributors, without whose ground-breaking work there would be nothing to recount.

Special thanks go to our editor, Mary Gentile, and our editors and publishers at Routledge.

We are grateful to our colleagues, who offered special insight, including: Professor David Rosenberg, director of the Zicklin Center for Corporate Integrity at City University of New York (CUNY) Baruch College, which hosted the 2017 panel discussion that led to this book; Professor Ester Fuchs, director of the Urban and Social Policy Program at Columbia University's School of International and Public Affairs; Professor Michael Gerrard, director of Columbia Law School's Sabin Center for Climate Change Law; Arthur T. Himmelman, collaboration consultant, formerly with the Hubert Humphrey School of Public Affairs at the University of Minnesota; Professor Yehuda Klein, chair of the economics department at CUNY's Brooklyn College; Jacqueline Klopp, director of Columbia's Center for Sustainable Urban Development; Professor Jeffrey Sachs of Columbia University, global director of the Sustainable Development Solutions Network (SDSN), and Jessica Espey, senior advisor at SDSN; Gavin Schmidt, climate researcher at NASA's Earth Sciences Division of the Goddard Institute for Space Studies; Peggy Shepard, cofounder and executive director, and Cecil Corbin Mark, deputy director, of WE ACT for Environmental Justice; Professor Charles Vorosmarty, director of the Environmental Sciences Initiative at CUNY's Advanced Science Research Center; and our students throughout the years at Columbia University, CUNY, SciencesPo, and elsewhere. We are also appreciative of the many dedicated staff from the New York City Mayor's office and agencies, without whom OneNYC would not have been developed and implemented, along with all those who contributed to the collaborative projects highlighted in the chapters.

Our gratitude also goes out to our countless colleagues, friends, and family around the globe who offered invaluable wisdom and support in manifold ways, including graphics assistance by Marina Seyffert.

Special thanks go to Nilda's daughters, Marina and Amalie, representing all youth, who, by their very being, offer hope and inspiration for our common future.

Introduction

It has become increasingly clear that no one sector, much less one individual or even organization, can approach the overarching threat of climate change alone without the cooperation of all.

When it comes to climate, there is an ever more pressing need to learn to get along to achieve results. The last few years have seen the disappearance of US federal leadership on climate change. In its wake has appeared a growing number of new climate allies (such as cities, states, business, and other institutions, including the military)—with new potential partners every day—seeking to mitigate growing climate impacts. That means better understanding of the incentives and rewards that motivate others, their needs and constraints, and the ways they operate and think. It also means developing an appreciation of what they bring to the table, including disparate points of view and training. When this book was conceived, the topic of exactly how to work together effectively—rather than why—had yet to be addressed head-on by authors examining the increasingly urgent need for mitigation, resilience, and adaptation to climate change. This book aims to illustrate ways in which people from disparate fields and points of view are cooperating to address climate issues at the ground level.

A key conclusion from Ann Goodman's book, *Adapting to Change: The Business of Climate Resilience* (Goodman, 2016), is that, to tackle daunting tasks, like climate resilience, we have to learn to cooperate, collaborate, and generally work better together. No sooner had the book been published in the wake of the 2015 Paris Conference of the Parties (COP21) than the US presidential election took place, creating a new political climate. Afterwards, grappling with climate change took on new urgency, as federal agencies stepped back and the government repealed regulations and issued edicts that stood to harm the environment. Adding to the urgency of tackling climate change are seemingly ubiquitous and proliferating extreme climate-related conditions and events—storms, floods, wildfires, and droughts—which also pose threats that disparate partners increasingly recognize they must approach collectively to protect humankind and the planet alike. Yet, on the plus side, the viscerally

DOI: 10.4324/9780429281242-1

recognizable changing climate in virtually all parts of the world can be seen as an opportunity for potential partners to acknowledge their commonality and come together to protect us all.

Supporters of our environmental well-being and climate—including cities, states, business, academia, the military, community-based organizations, and religious organizations—are awakening and mobilizing. They understand both the imminent and long-term risks of climate deterioration and the advantages of addressing them now. The challenge of climate change goes beyond past efforts at collective institutional initiatives as seen in traditional public-private partnerships (sometimes called PPPs) and the four Ps, public-private-philanthropic partnerships (though such partnerships are essential to building climate resilience). Instead, we still must learn some essential lessons about working together, despite the wondrous technologies and other innovations humans continue to devise. Indeed, this apparently ever-broader-based acknowledgment of the need to act may hasten action.

Examples of such efforts are proliferating. Locally generated grassroots activities based on horizontal networks are educating their communities and gaining support from the business sector for climate and resiliency action. These networks are flat rather than hierarchical structures, often formed with a combination of new and old organizations, and include participants who have not been active on climate or local issues in the past. Business leaders are developing new types of social ventures based on finding shared economic gains that also support social and environmental goals, including climate.

Perhaps nowhere is this phenomenon more visible than in the growing cooperation between companies and cities, as these institutions increasingly begin to collaborate to deter and prepare for climate disasters and the potentially deadly effects of storms and floods that have already affected coastal and other regions. No less affected are the companies that both need and support cities, from the customers they serve in growing urban areas to the employees they rely on to operate.

Such cooperation is increasingly evident, urgent, and necessary, as the urban population grows worldwide and as, in the cases presented here in the United States, the joint interests of cities, states, and businesses are progressively intertwined. For the first time, subnational organizations, such as C40, UN Habitat, ICLEI–Local Governments for Sustainability, and the Under2 Coalition, played a major role in the run up to the Paris Climate Agreement, and they continue to show how collaboration transcending past institutional barriers is a powerful force in the energy transition that can mitigate climate change.[1] For example, US governors, mayors, universities, and the private sector all responded quickly to the announcement that the United States would be withdrawing from the Paris Climate Agreement. We Are Still In and the Climate Alliance, formed by key governors, promised to adhere to the commitments regardless of federal action.[2] America's Pledge, which initially included 30 mayors, three governors, more than 100 companies (and, not insignificantly, 80 universities), was assembled in part by former New York City Mayor Michael Bloomberg and California Governor Jerry Brown to tally members' greenhouse gas emission reductions and report them to the United Nations. It has since grown to 2,700 signatories across the United States.[3] We see this hunger for cooperation echoing throughout the sustainability community.

At a discussion on how communities can create a resilience strategy at the Environmental Protection Agency's (EPA) annual Climate Leadership Conference in Chicago in early 2017, for instance, the conversation centered on cities and how they might better partner with the private sector. But the focus quickly turned to how these and the many other parties central to achieving climate resilience might work toward the common goal of addressing a shared threat. Since then, conversations and action have only escalated, reaching far beyond sustainability experts to ordinary people, who experience mounting climate disruption more frequently in their everyday lives. Notable among them are students—most famously Greta Thunberg and participants in School Strike for Climate, the Sunrise Movement, as well as decentralized movements such as Extinction Rebellion—who are protesting around the world.[4]

During New York City's Climate Week 2017, the City University of New York's (CUNY) Zicklin Center for Corporate Integrity at Baruch College sought to raise awareness of the urgent need to cooperate in slowing down climate change. Participating in this public panel were leaders from city government, a community organization, a multinational company, and the military.

Corroborating the fact that lay people are ever more concerned about the impact of climate change, the panel generated probing conversations during the question-and-answer period, with audience members engaging in lively discussion well beyond its end. That experience has been repeated in high-level conversations on climate resilience from Florida to Virginia to Paris to Bogota.[5] The evident thirst for more information, guidance, and examples of collaboration for climate resilience at that initial CUNY event in New York was the underpinning of and impetus for this book, with each panelist contributing a chapter, along with others later recruited to add breadth and depth to exploration of the topic.

As a result, this book centers on case studies (many still in the making) of how people work together for climate resilience and sustainability. Practitioners present stories from across a variety of fields—including city government, state regulators, business, finance, community and climate justice groups, the military, academia, and nonprofit organizations—about what it takes to make their initiatives successful. The stories allude to philanthropists, religious communities, engineers, and urbanists, along with world organizations such as the United Nations.

The cases underscore actions and strategies that worked, along with potential challenges and how they were avoided or overcome. The examples draw out principles that may help others from a variety of sectors work together to meet these challenges. These emerging guidelines for successful collaboration, collected in the concluding chapter, elucidate principles enunciated by experts who note that generally there is not as much cooperation as there should be.

This book demonstrates ways in which people from disparate fields can work together to address climate resilience specifically, an expertise that, as far as we know, does not yet exist. And as the chapters in this book corroborate, principles of collaboration from select experts tackling other issues may be adapted to facing climate resilience. Arthur T. Himmelman, a consultant formerly with the Hubert Humphrey School of Public Affairs at the University of Minnesota, suggests mutuality in three forms is helpful in partnerships: mutual respect, learning, and accountability for results.[6] This fundamental—if sometimes difficult to execute—suggestion is reflected in cases underpinning chapters in this book, including, especially, Chapter 2, focusing on communities; Chapter 4, on equity; and Chapter 6, on regional partnerships. But all, to one degree or another, exemplify how mutual respect, continual learning, and accountability facilitate the collaborative process.

Effective collaboration is complicated by the struggle for power, as Himmelman points out. A barrier to achieving collaborative relationships in climate and many other areas is unequal power among partners. In working for a common purpose, Himmelman suggests viewing power as the capacity to produce intended results, instead of the ability to dominate and control. Such power battles hinder cooperation and partnership, in the climate arena specifically, as Gavin Schmidt, a climate researcher at NASA's Earth Sciences Division of the Goddard Institute for Space Studies noted in a 2018 talk at CUNY's Graduate Center. Schmidt talked of "politicized science," which can occur "when scientific results appear to impact vested political, ethical, or economic interests." In such cases, like climate denial, "New results are only seen in the public realm to the extent that they project onto the political/ethical/economic question," Schmidt noted. Again, specifically pertaining to climate change, the preference in the public discourse to be overly focused on technicalities can often be traced to what Schmidt called "scientized politics," which can occur "when advocates turn to science in order to avoid debating the values that underlie their positions."

To avoid such clashes in climate collaboration, parties in cases illustrated in this book sought from the beginning to find ways and even words to help people work together on finding common ground on a complex and potentially contentious issue. Particularly notable are steps by city leaders (Chapter 1), communities (Chapter 2), and business (Chapter 5) to enlist cooperation from parties who might potentially push back at working toward climate resilience, try to understand their reluctance, help train them for mutual aims, and even select or omit specific words that might produce volatile or hostile reactions from partners essential to achieving successful collaborative action.

Finally, this book seeks to inspire readers—business and public-policy students, academics, practitioners, and others with a keen interest in the growing need for collaboration on this urgent threat—by highlighting cases that have succeeded, building and expanding on cases featured in Goodman (2016) and the 2017 Climate Week CUNY panel (Baruch College Zicklin Center for Corporate Integrity, 2017).

As more parties become involved in climate solutions, no one solution fits all situations, needs, or participants in any project. Much depends on the scope of the project, the players, the immediate and long-term goals, the outcomes desired, and the roles to be played by parties in the collaborative process. As the chapter authors point out, it helps to discuss such issues in advance and remain open to—and even anticipate—potential modifications as the process evolves.

Moreover, as more sectors become involved in the process, our cases make clear the need for understanding what each sector offers, what each might learn from others, what each needed and wanted in cases they experienced or led, and what each has learned. The end goal is to help readers understand how to approach this communal problem together and formulate how they may be able—with others—to tackle the looming climate crisis.

The chapters in this book, briefly outlined below, illustrate approaches from a variety of parties already seeking ways to collaborate for climate resilience. While these projects may start at the local level, they all acknowledge a need for global cooperation; some, in fact, already incorporate international themes, principles, or players. As the chapter titles suggest, they offer ideas from key parties involved in achieving climate resilience.

Chapter 1: Cities and climate resilience (NYC Office of Sustainability)

In 2015, New York City Mayor Bill de Blasio launched OneNYC, the long-term sustainability plan for the city. In keeping with the newly elected mayor's focus on economic and social inequality and his concern for the climate, the definition of "sustainability" for the plan was broadened from previous plans to more closely parallel classic sustainable development parameters for NYC. To develop the plan, more than 70 city agencies were brought together, along with a Sustainability Advisory Board representing multiple city sectors, elected officials, and city residents.

Since the United Nations was in the final stages of developing its international Sustainable Development Goals (SDGs), OneNYC was developed in accordance with those goals as well. Hence, OneNYC was positioned to demonstrate how cities' sustainability goals could track with the global SDGs and how they could strengthen each other as they sought to achieve similar aims.

An important component of the plan proposed cutting 80 percent of greenhouse gas (GHG) emissions by 2050, focusing initially on buildings as about 70 percent of NYC's GHG emissions come from buildings. A separate technical working group followed up on the initial OneNYC planning and devised a thorough strategy toward meeting this goal.

Chapter 2: Communities: Teaming up with companies, cities, states, academia (The RAFT)

A US region especially vulnerable to sea level rise and related factors is coastal Virginia. As in NYC, in 2015 three Virginia universities created The Resilience Adaptation Feasibility Tool (The RAFT), a project that brought together representatives from localities to brainstorm ways to help them become more resilient to rising seas and recurrent flooding.

The project differs in three ways from other self-scoring "report card" assessments: (1) It represents a long-term collaboration among universities, an unusual achievement in itself; (2) rather than "self-grading" community resilience efforts, it relies on an outside independent collaborative team from the three universities to assess environmental, social, and social resilience conditions according to a consistent set of terms and metrics; (3) The RAFT is "full-service" in that, after giving a locality its scorecard, a team works with the locality to develop a checklist of actions and advises on strategies and actions for improvement over the next year.

The RAFT learned that "one size doesn't fit all." Localities in the area differ in their economic and geographic characteristics, and the localities themselves worked on identifying the varying needs and priorities. The RAFT also learned the importance of remaining flexible in adapting and administering their assessment tool with a focus on making it possible to avoid divisions over political views about climate change.

Part of The RAFT's continuing success is an evolving element of expanding circles of partnership with academia, non-governmental organizations (NGOs), the private sector (including local businesses, environmental, and engineering consulting firms), and government, acknowledging the need to leverage expertise beyond the core collaborative team.

Chapter 3: Climate change and national security: Opportunities for learning and cooperation

In recent decades, the national security community, including the US Department of Defense (DoD), has taken a serious look at the implications of climate change, especially as it might affect or relate to national security. This chapter looks at three specific cases: the US Navy's Task Force Climate Change and climate change in the Arctic; the threat that sea level rise poses to installations and the military's mission in the Hampton Roads region of Virginia; and climate change education in the curriculum at the US Military Academy at West Point.

The examples illustrate different points: the first provides a success story of interagency and international cooperation, with clear outcomes and an enduring legacy; the second is an ongoing story with no clear way forward, many challenges, and opportunities for cooperation; the third is an illustration of how an organization is equipping its future leaders with the knowledge and tools to lead in a complex world, ready to face and solve the challenges of tomorrow, understanding the potential impact of a changing climate on the mission of the armed forces, at home and abroad.

The three examples offer a glimpse of different ways the DoD, in partnership with others, including scientists and foreign governments, has studied and planned for a changing climate. Each case illustrates how groups or organizations took a *long view* of a complex problem, identified possible solutions, and remained patient and persistent in working toward those solutions. Each example also shows the importance of *leadership*: individuals or small groups determined to steer their organization(s) and, in many cases, reach across boundaries to collaborate and assist in identifying and solving complex problems.

Chapter 4: Equity: Climate justice in Detroit

In 2009, chapter author Kimberly Hill Knott joined the nonprofit organization Detroiters Working for Environmental Justice (DWEJ). After attending the Conference of the Parties (COP15) in Copenhagen, Denmark, that year, she saw a need to create Detroit's first Climate Action Plan.

In 2012, when Detroit was on the verge of bankruptcy and was appointing an emergency manager, DWEJ launched the Detroit Climate Action Collaborative (DCAC). DCAC's plan included 11 phases: (1) structural development, (2) research—ongoing, (3) fundraising—ongoing, (4) community and sector engagement—partnership development, (5) idea exchange, (6) framework development, (7) marketing—ongoing, (8) writing, (9) reviewing, (10) launch, and (11) implementation.

Recognizing from the start that it would be essential to involve many partners in the ambitious undertaking, the group enlisted a professor from the University of Michigan to lead a steering committee and created five working groups: Homes and Neighborhoods; Solid Waste; Public Health; Parks, Public Spaces, and Water Infrastructure; and Businesses and Institutions. By the end, more than 25 organizations contributed to the effort.

From conducting initial research to raising funds to making a film, the grassroots organization eventually created a plan that has played an important role in addressing climate change and has provided a model for other communities seeking greater equity in climate change initiatives.

Chapter 5: Business: Building climate-resilient supply chains (IBM supply chain)

Throughout its history of advancing environmental performance, IBM has recognized the need to encourage its suppliers to pursue a similar course. A company can set high goals, but to achieve a sustainable supply chain—and overall sustainability goals—suppliers and partners must do the same. No company is an island, so business collaboration is key, no less in the area of corporate responsibility than in others. To this end, IBM has collaborated internally and externally to establish programs that address social and environmental aspects of its supply chain, including climate protection. In this chapter, two programs are highlighted: (1) IBM's deployment of the Electronic Industry Citizenship Coalition (now Responsible Business Alliance) Code of Conduct, which started as an internal IBM initiative, expanded to the wider electronics industry, and eventually moved beyond the electronics industry; and (2) IBM's Social and Environmental Management System supplier requirements, which has included, from the outset, a strong focus on training IBM sourcing staff and the company's suppliers.

While the benefits—to IBM as well as supplier companies—are great, there are also challenges, from lack of awareness and understanding by external suppliers, especially in growth market countries, to suppliers that categorically think the mandates do not apply to them. Further, the scale of a global enterprise with large numbers of employees and suppliers poses its own challenge. IBM addresses these challenges with strong support at the executive level and reaches down to regional procurement levels to drive performance and compliance, with a focus on education for IBM sourcing staff and suppliers.

Chapter 6: Regional deals, international players

In the absence of federal action, among the most successful public initiatives on climate change are those from US states, which have formed coalitions to reduce greenhouse gas emissions. Following the failed 2010 congressional attempt to create a federal cap-and-trade market, two regional market-based systems were formed: the Regional Greenhouse Gas Initiative (RGGI), which formally began in 2009 and is a partnership of 11 northeast and mid-Atlantic states, and the Western Climate Initiative (WCI), a partnership between California and the Canadian province of Quebec, which held its first joint auction in 2014.

States have found other ways to collaborate on climate change, as well. Another high-profile example is collaboration among progressive state attorneys general (AGs). In recent years, state AGs have increasingly acted in concert to push for affirmative steps to reduce GHG emissions and oppose attempts by the Trump administration to roll back rules and regulations intended to address climate change and reduce GHG emissions.

On June 1, 2017, when President Donald J. Trump announced that he would pull the United States out of the Paris Climate Agreement, the governors of New York, California, and Washington issued statements announcing that they were forming a new state coalition called the United States Climate Alliance to address climate change through policy initiatives. Given that climate change is a global problem, it is promising that Mexico and Canada were involved with the Alliance's announcements, collectively committing, for example, to reach 50 percent zero-carbon power generation across North America by 2025 (United States Climate Alliance, n.d.).

In sum, the different voices across and within each chapter demonstrate that multiple views must be included—and even welcomed—into the climate conversation to achieve resilience. Cases explored in these chapters include examples ranging from city government to citizen action groups to the armed forces to companies around the world. The players in these pages—reflecting different personalities, approaches, and special challenges—suggest the need for multiple voices to tackle the climate challenge, locally and globally.

References

Baruch College Center for Corporate Integrity. "Learning to Play in the Sandbox: Cooperating for Climate Resilience," September 19, 2017. https://baruch.mediaspace.kaltura.com/media/1_9qvxkv5p.

Goodman, Ann. *Adapting to Change: The Business of Climate Resilience*. New York: Business Expert Press, 2016.

United States Climate Alliance. "International Cooperation," n.d., accessed June 29, 2019. https://www.usclimatealliance.org/international-cooperation/.

Notes

1   More information may be found on the websites of the referenced organizations: https://www.c40.org/, https://unhabitat.org/un-habitat-at-a-glance/, https://www.iclei.org/, and https://www.under2coalition.org/.

2   https://www.wearestillin.com/, https://www.climatealliance.org/home.html.

3   https://www.americaspledgeonclimate.com/.

4   https://www.rollingstone.com/culture/culture-features/the-new-eco-radicals-966441/.

5   Goodman was a keynote speaker, along with Lester Brown, at the 10th Annual International Conference of CEID (Centro de Estudios para el Desarrollo Sostenible) in Bogota, where the Spanish edition of her first book, *Adapting to Change*, was launched in Spanish. At the 2017 6th International Network of Tropical Architecture Conference (Tropical Storms as a Setting for Adaptive Development and Architecture), Goodman was invited to the University of Florida to run a plenary session entitled Storm of Opportunity: Business Models and Urban Resilience. Goodman served as a keynote speaker at the 29th Annual Environment Virginia Symposium at the Virginia Military Institute in 2018.

6   Himmelman's work can be accessed at https://www.himmelmanconsulting.com.

Chapter 1

Cities and climate resilience (NYC Office of Sustainability)

Nilda Mesa

New York and OneNYC: climate and sustainability planning

New York City has been one of the world's leaders on climate policy and practice dating back to at least 2007, when Mayor Michael Bloomberg and his administration released PlaNYC (City of New York, 2007), the city's long-term sustainability plan. That plan was spurred in large part by data showing the city's population was projected to increase dramatically, along with a concern that the city's quality of life and infrastructure would be overwhelmed and suffer without sufficient goals, programs, and metrics to preserve and enhance them.

In 2015, under newly elected Mayor Bill de Blasio, the city took another leap, calling for reducing carbon emissions by 80 percent by 2050 and updating its long-term sustainability plan to include the new target. OneNYC (City of New York, 2015), as the new plan was named, also expanded the scope of PlaNYC significantly. It was the first comprehensive major city sustainability plan to adopt the United Nations' definition of sustainability, which includes social, economic, and environmental considerations. The methodology included approaching sustainability as a design and systems problem, and in so doing involved more than 70 citywide agencies, multiple stakeholders, academics, elected officials, and residents in a complicated and multilayered collaboration.

Throughout the course of the next few years, the city tiered its collaborations and designed strategies for specific goals and visions, turning them into data-based policies and legislation with the flexibility and technical depth to begin to tackle the city's ambitious climate goals.

This collaborative and design thinking process, as described below, even with a few fits and starts, advanced sustainability and climate policy, as well as practice, and set a new standard for other cities.

DOI: 10.4324/9780429281242-2

Background

New York City's Charter requires the city to complete a long-term sustainability plan every four years, with annual progress reports in the intervening years. The plan must include:

> an identification and analysis of long-term planning and sustainability issues associated with, but not limited to, housing, open space, brownfields, transportation, water quality and infrastructure, air quality, energy, and climate change…
>
> (City of New York, 2004)

The Charter also requires that the plan contain goals, policies, programs, and milestones to meet the objectives and mandates consultations with a sustainability advisory board and the public. In 2015, following 2012's Hurricane Sandy, the Charter added that the plan must "include a list of policies, programs and actions that the city will seek to implement or undertake to achieve each goal relating to the resiliency of critical infrastructure, the built environment, coastal protection and communities" (ibid.).

While the language makes plain what must be in the plans, it does not direct a specific process or limit future directors of the Office of Long-Term Planning and Sustainability (OLTPS) from adding new items. The Charter gives mayors great flexibility in developing their management processes and goals within a framework of some transparency. The one hard-and-fast rule is that the plan and updates must be transmitted to the mayor and the city council speaker by Earth Day, or April 22.

Under Mayor Bloomberg's watch, the Departments of Environmental Protection, Sanitation, Parks, Planning, Transportation, Citywide and Administrative Services, and the Office of Environmental Remediation were assigned the development of PlaNYC sections and chapters, categories that corresponded to those in the city's Charter, under the supervision and direction of OLTPS. However, there was little interaction among the agencies in developing the sections of the plan; rather, the agencies' assignments were limited to their traditional agency scope. The PlaNYC participants consulted regularly and often early on with the Sustainability Advisory Board, made up largely of environmental advocates and civic and business organizations. As the years went by, consultations occurred less regularly.

There were several key advantages and disadvantages to this approach. Clear lines of authority and accountability from the start of the process meant that there was little ambiguity as to who was responsible for delivering what and when, a mark of Bloomberg's private-sector-honed management style. Agencies by and large had to use their existing budgets, which kept down costs, even as it discouraged expansive costly initiatives. In several instances, such as with the popular Million Trees Initiative, the city received outside funding to supplement agency budgets.

With a limited number of agencies tapped, management and implementation of the plan appeared to be relatively straightforward, which was important to ensure that the goals and programs would be delivered, and measuring how well they were working. Agencies did not necessarily understand the larger picture, however, or know the synergies they might share with other agencies. They stated that they felt disconnected, a bit isolated from the development of broader citywide goals, and constrained from seeking funds for initiatives in addition to their already-programmed work.

Nonetheless, the Bloomberg era PlaNYC reports redefined for New York, and many cities, how sustainability could be integrated and implemented in a largely post-industrial urban environment. The Bloomberg team's vision that gritty Gotham could somehow be a center for environmental innovation positioned the city as a leader, confounded skeptics, and challenged other large metropolises worldwide to meet the new standard.

OneNYC 2015

Mayor de Blasio took office in January 2014, after running on a platform that New York had become "a tale of two cities" (Walker, 2013). In the years since the first PlaNYC, New York's population and economy had grown, but so had economic inequality and housing costs. Through de Blasio's first year in office, many of the environmental advocates who had come to have confidence in the Bloomberg approach were skeptical that the new mayor shared their commitment to sustainability. The Earth Day deadline loomed in April 2015. In December, I was brought on board as the first director of the Mayor's Office of Sustainability, which merged OLTPS with the Office of Environmental Cooperation, and we assembled a team to put together a new long-term sustainability plan for the city.

In keeping with the new mayor's focus on economic inequality, as well as his language on climate, affordable housing, pre-kindergarten education, and other priorities, the mayor agreed that the definition of sustainability for the new plan should be broadened to more closely parallel classic sustainable development parameters, applied and reinvented for New York City. While there are many definitions of sustainability, the city relied upon the UN's Brundtland Commission definition: "Sustainable development is development that meets the needs of the present without compromising the ability of future generations to meet their own needs" (Brundtland Commission, 1987).

These were uncharted waters for New York City. A new strategy was called for to hammer out the framework, goals, programs, and policies to deliver this sustainable development focus within less than four months while complying with the New York City Charter. That new strategy was to build a broad internal and external network, using design thinking and systems approaches to develop the visions, goals, and initiatives that would make it all happen for the next four years and beyond.

For a number of years before founding the Mayor's Office of Sustainability and serving as its director, I developed a graduate capstone class at Columbia University's School of International and Public Affairs that experimented with a design thinking approach to solving real-life issues for public sector clients. Design thinking is based on Roger Martin's business theories, particularly as described in *The Design of Business* (2009), and promulgated by the industrial design firm IDEO.

The design thinking method sets up a circular design process that starts with gathering information, brainstorming without judgment, testing ideas, incorporating feedback from end users and other stakeholders, and improving the original design. It is a logical way to frame a policymaking, business, or product design process, though it is not especially well known among climate policymakers. I used similar circular approaches in previous work at the federal level, working through the often stilted environmental review process to achieve consensus and satisfactory results across multiple stakeholders and governments. Design thinking has been used in business for years, but not to develop urban sustainability plans.

In addition, as I will describe, I incorporated ideas into the internal city process from Donella Meadows's *Thinking in Systems* (2008), which unpacks often invisible interrelationships and structures and how they affect each other as part of a complex system. New York City, to my knowledge, had never before explicitly used design and systems thinking approaches to tackle a complex and newly defined sustainability matrix.

During the first year of the de Blasio administration, city agency senior leaders identified cohesive themes and values, based largely on campaign commitments, that would define the new administration's priorities. They developed eight themes, grounded in a consensus across the administration. These themes became the initial foundation for our endeavor, with the understanding that they would most likely change over the course of the sustainability-planning process. They provided the draft framework for analyzing and designing around the main themes within a system. The themes included climate, health care, education, poverty, affordable housing, crime, and resiliency.

By late fall 2014, an internal steering committee took shape. It was led by the first deputy mayor and included the deputy mayor for Strategic Policy Initiatives, director of Operations, City Planning director and chair of the Planning Commission, deputy director of the Office of Management and Budget, the mayor's special advisor on Infrastructure, director of Resiliency, and me, the director of the Mayor's Office of Sustainability, also serving as project director for OneNYC.

The kickoff meeting in early January 2015 called together the heads of city agencies with other key senior leaders in the administration and was led by the mayor. Members of the Steering Committee presented information on past plans as well as current and initial projections of conditions. The work ahead for the plan was framed thus: New York City, founded in 1625, would celebrate its 400th anniversary in 10 years. What would the city need in the next 10 years to position itself for the next century: not just what was under the city's jurisdiction, but more broadly, what would be necessary for the city to thrive?

This formulation was important: the plan would not be limited to a narrow scope within agencies but would look at the system as a whole, at its interlocking elements, and identify those parts of the system that were critical to meeting city aims to thrive and grow in the years to come. Once those puzzle pieces were defined, the city could then develop a strategy. Figure 1.1 illustrates the challenges and opportunities of the transition to OneNYC.

Using this overarching question, agency heads and their senior leaders were handed stacks of sticky-note pads. Posters with data and key information, organized according to the eight consensus themes developed throughout the year, were positioned around the large hall. Agency leaders circulated to stop at each themed station, for three minutes as timed by a bell, and scribbled their ideas to improve city life as fast as they could, with one idea per note. Agency officials were told that the notes would be anonymous and to offer their ideas not in their capacity as heads of agencies but rather from their expertise on the city and in policy making. Outside-of-the-box thinking was encouraged. Participants were assured that there would be no consequences for putting in their ideas, and the more ideas they wrote the better. The typically risk-averse agency leaders had free rein to be creative and forward-thinking, regardless of

Core challenges and opportunities

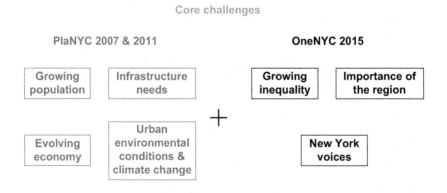

Figure 1.1 Core challenges and opportunities
Source: Office of the Mayor, 2015

their usual day-to-day constraints. The three-minute limit and the call for speed and quantity was also meant to bypass any undermining internal criticisms that something might sound too ambitious.

By the end of the afternoon, thousands of yellow sticky notes had been placed. These thousands of ideas were assembled and organized, and became the clay from which OneNYC was sculpted. In addition, a tight timeline was laid out with specific working group and agency deliverables. It was apparent to all that the months ahead would require a massive citywide effort, and the process sought the input and expertise of all the agencies to put together the draft. Agency leaders understood that they were part of something bold and potentially transformative, and that the process would rely upon their expertise and, ultimately, their ability to implement the initiatives. This non-linear process was unlike any they had seen before, and they wanted to be part of it.

The eight themes were developed into domains to be expanded upon by the interagency working groups. The domains were: core infrastructure and services, diverse and inclusive government, economic security and mobility, education, empowered residents and civic engagement, health and well-being, housing, and personal and community safety. The domains became the organizing structure for the interagency working groups, which took the anonymous ideas generated by commissioners and senior agency leaders in the initial kickoff as their starting point.

Each working group was co-chaired by two different agencies that had primary responsibility for the themed subject matter. Representing the agencies as co-chairs were senior administration members from the agencies and relevant City Hall offices who had enough authority to be able to speak for their agencies. Significantly, they included a mix of political and civil servants to ensure the right blend of institutional knowledge with policy direction. Figure 1.2 maps the structure of the team involved.

The members of the working groups often included agency representatives who had never met and had little or no idea that another agency was working on similar goals within their themes. Consultants provided additional analytical and quantitative support. Opportunities for joint efforts were identified in many instances, while the close and demanding working conditions brought together agencies that in the past may have seen each other's efforts as working at cross-purposes but now found common ground. The working groups met separately, submitting their draft analyses and ideas to the core steering committee weekly. We were able to identify where working groups were developing ideas that overlapped for further study and development. In addition, several participants sat on more than one of the working groups.

These groups were tasked with coming up with recommendations for the steering committee on the plan's visions and goals, along with the policy proposals, potential funding sources, targets, and metrics. All funding would be vetted with the budget office as part of the budget process. The working groups would be charged with writing the drafts for senior review. All proposals were

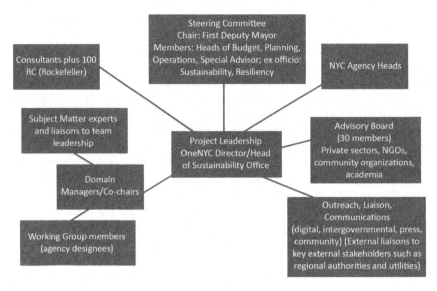

Figure 1.2 OneNYC team structure diagram
Source: the author

required to propose budget estimates and sources of funding in order to make it to the final rounds of review. All proposals were required to supply relevant metrics and indicators to ensure accountability as well as assess progress and impacts early on after implementation.

The groups themselves operated by consensus, though not necessarily unanimity. In other words, it was enough for the vast majority of participants to agree that something could move forward, and the goal was for a collegial and constructive process rather than a contentious power game. This approach eased the flow of ideas and encouraged collaboration and negotiation to reach timeline goals. If a working group lacked consensus, it could not include the proposal. However, no one agency could block a proposal that had the agreement of the others. We stipulated that "Vegas rules" applied: whatever discussion took place in the working sessions, stayed in the working sessions, and was not to be used against members at a future date.

Members of the steering committee, senior city leaders, and I reviewed drafts throughout the process, and we asked the groups questions and gave input. Communications were frequent with the working groups. I led daily meetings with steering committee designees and at least weekly meetings with the steering committee principals. We kept a tight watch on the schedule, deliverables, and supplemental economic and planning analyses by outside consultants. The alchemy happened when we put senior agency experts in the same room, gave them tight deadlines, held them accountable, and conducted senior reviews. They knew their expertise and creativity were crucial to the whole plan, and they rose to the occasion. Agency heads made the process a priority, as it was clear it was a mayoral priority. In fact, as requests for information and input filtered through and across agencies with every week, more agency experts called to volunteer their time, asking to be put on working groups where they thought their agency had a piece that could complete the puzzle.

As the interagency working groups were making progress, we assembled the Sustainability Advisory Board and launched an effort to include expertise and input from outside of the administration. The new advisory board added several new sectors to its membership, including tech, hospitals, foundations, labor, social services, resiliency, and small business. Special sessions were held with private sector companies with large operations in New York, such as UPS, Google, and Etsy, and with elected officials. These sessions were invaluable to test ideas and assumptions and gain insight from the participants' experience and knowledge. For example, these sessions spotlighted that both the cost and availability of childcare and broadband speeds were seen as obstacles for businesses seeking to grow and stay in the city.

An interactive workshop allowed agency working groups to brainstorm and test draft ideas and findings to date, benefiting from advisory group members' expertise and proposals, which the working group members then took back to their own sessions. Through citywide emails, surveys, and polling, we tested ideas with residents and invited them to name their own priorities for the city's new long-term plan. These inputs led the agency working groups to reevaluate and change proposals, identifying, for example, issues such as internet speed and childcare as obstacles to city sustainability, while confirming others: for example, housing costs and commuting times.

At the same time, the United Nations was in the final stages of developing the Sustainable Development Goals (SDGs), which were due for a vote in September 2015 (United Nations, n.d.). This complex multinational negotiation produced 17 goals, all of which were consistent with OneNYC goals. The OneNYC team kept an eye on the likely direction of the negotiations and benefited from the input of Sustainability Advisory Board Co-chair Jeffrey Sachs, who was integral to the UN process.

As a result, OneNYC was positioned to demonstrate how a city's sustainability goals could track with the global goals of the SDGs, and how they could strengthen each other as they sought to achieve similar goals. When the SDGs were adopted by 184 countries in September 2015, OneNYC could demonstrate New York City's path toward these goals, aiming to be a model for others. In addition, the SDGs even in draft form provided much-needed cross-checking for the development of OneNYC, providing a global context and helping identify possible gaps and common areas.

After much rewriting and negotiation, within a few months, hundreds of consensus-based proposals emerged, grounded in expertise and with potential funding sources identified, for steering committee review. Each group was proud of its proposals, with a sense of ownership and advocacy for its programs and OneNYC, which lasted well into the following years of agency implementation.

The last stages of the OneNYC process put the final touches on synchronizing the plan with the independently developed annual city poverty report, the 10-year capital plan, and the annual budget process. In addition, the proposals developed by the working groups overlapped and interlinked in many cases, showing the need to draw them together yet more tightly. We observed that our goals were even more interrelated than we had expected, and we synthesized the original eight themes into four overarching visions for the city: growth, equity, sustainability, and resiliency. Each vision served a double duty: first as the organizing principle for the goals and initiatives, and second, as a tool to layer over the proposals to scrub them for missed opportunities for co-benefits as well as any hidden conflicts or inconsistencies. Where the visions included previously announced priorities—such as the goal to cut 80 percent of the city's greenhouse gas (GHG) emissions by 2050, VisionZero's goal to have zero pedestrian fatalities, or affordable-housing goals—OneNYC fleshed them out after benefiting from the 360° view from the interagency working groups and outside input.

The collaborative ideal extended to our anticipated readers. We placed an emphasis on making the plan readable, engaging, and accessible to the average New Yorker. We did not want the plan to sit on a shelf, as so many do, of interest only to policy wonks. We knew that many would be looking at the plan online, so we designed a distinct online version that would invite comments and allow residents to jump to the sections they were most interested in for a deep dive or just to look at the overall setup for an overview. The more traditional form was printed and bound as a book but could also be accessed in PDF format via the website. The mayor's launch was widely publicized and covered by the city's media.

Throughout, an emphasis on data and analysis, carrying on and expanding the practices already developed under the Bloomberg administration, provided a shared language and view of the city that allowed participants to contribute their expertise and evaluate what had already been developed. The quest to get the data and analysis right, with the willingness to evaluate and revise, led to a pathbreaking shift in urban sustainability policymaking, as reflected in the city's modifications to its budget and planning processes in subsequent years to include evaluations using the four lenses and visions. The annual progress reports measured the status of the proposals, in some cases eliminating programs that were found to be infeasible. More than 300 scholarly articles in the last five years refer to OneNYC, evidence of its place in the development of sustainability planning.

Agencies led the implementation. They developed in more detail the initiatives identified in the original OneNYC and published their own reports and detailed goals. These agencies included the Department of Sanitation, which took an aggressive stance toward diverting waste from landfills. The Department of Transportation pursued its VisionZero plan, to cut pedestrian fatalities from vehicles, under the auspices of OneNYC. That department also undertook a massive effort to restripe streets, provide more car-free zones, and increase miles of bicycle paths to encourage multi-modal transportation. The Department of Citywide Administrative Services developed its strategy for transforming the city's vehicle fleet into a largely electric fleet, which is well underway. The subsequent plan, four years later, carried forward most of the programs and goals, though some were more modest, and provided detailed and comprehensive information regarding how OneNYC was implemented (City of New York, 2015).

Data and buildings climate policy: the road to climate legislation

Of the many efforts that tiered off from OneNYC, one of the most important and technically difficult was how to cut greenhouse gas (GHG) emissions from New York City's 1 million buildings. In 2014, de Blasio announced a goal to cut citywide GHG emissions by 80 percent by 2050. OneNYC set up a framework to develop a detailed and substantive strategy.

Annual GHG emissions inventories for the last eight years consistently showed that approximately 70–71 percent of the city's emissions came from buildings and the energy supplied to them, 20 percent from transportation, and 7 percent from waste. New Yorkers' emissions per capita were about one-third of the US average, yet overall emissions were still significant, making up approximately 40 percent of New York State's total share. The city's emissions profile was markedly different from other cities, which were more evenly divided between buildings and transportation (except for Los Angeles, where mild weather and its dependence on cars meant transportation made up the majority of emissions).

At the same time, the percentage of renewable energy going into the city's grid was less than 5 percent. Based on the data, it was clear that the biggest opportunity to cut emissions would be from buildings. The devastation of Hurricane Sandy and the work of the New York City Panel on Climate Change made it clear that, as a coastal city, New York was vulnerable to flooding and other climate effects in the decades to come.

In early 2015, the Mayor's Office of Sustainability (MOS) established a Buildings Technical Working Group (BTWG) to tackle the next stage (City of New York, 2016). Approximately 50 external members participated. The stakeholders selected included those with expertise on buildings and energy as well as representatives of key groups. Overall, they represented the real-estate industry, affordable-housing developers, utilities, environmental advocates, architects, labor organizations, engineers, the construction industry, commercial- and residential-building owners, foundations, and the New York City green building and finance community. City agencies with responsibility over portfolios of buildings, such as the Departments of Housing Preservation and Development; Buildings; Citywide Administrative Services; School Construction Authority; and Design and Construction, were also included, as was the New York City Council Speaker's Office.

Throughout the course of the next year, MOS conducted a series of analyses based on data that the city had been collecting since 2009 from buildings larger than 50,000 square feet, which are required to complete benchmarking and energy audits annually to help the building sector manage energy use and understand the performance of specific building systems. The data allowed the city to identify energy-use patterns and typologies of the most common buildings in the city. The draft analyses were presented to the BTWG during the year, and several working groups homed in on more specific issues. Having data that was reliable and comprehensive was a key factor for the BTWG's work to proceed.

When MOS released the final report in 2016, it marked a significant advance in the city's understanding of the systems and building types that made up the emissions profile. The information identified the city's eight most common building typologies, based on age, use and size, and it highlighted the most likely and cost-effective strategic pathways to achieve carbon-emissions reductions by building type. The report also listed a series of administrative and legislative proposals that would mark the next steps. The proposals incorporated BTWG member input in significant ways, noting, for example, the necessity to time building improvements to capital cycles to reduce the burden on building owners.

While the analyses were by and large adopted by consensus, the next steps were ultimately opposed by some members of the BTWG, namely the real-estate industry and some building owners. The BTWG was formally disbanded, yet its members continued to pursue solutions to the issues raised in other venues during that year. Throughout the next few years, another working group was convened by one of the members, an outside nonprofit organization, the Urban Green Council, which sought to resolve outstanding issues. The mayor's office and the city council also developed and circulated several versions of a building emissions bill, with the original version languishing.

In 2019, the city council finalized a package of eight bills that put together financing, advisory support, phased building energy-performance standards, and a future rulemaking and adjudicative process, and allowed alternative means of compliance for special categories of buildings such as affordable housing, hospitals, and places of worship. Despite the objections of segments of the real-estate industry, which proposed a different approach, the council passed the Climate Mobilization Act in April 2019 (New York City Council, n.d.), making New York City's buildings larger than 25,000 square feet subject to phased carbon-emissions caps.

After years of working groups, analyses, and negotiations—and despite the opposition of some stakeholders—this package became, to date, the US's most comprehensive buildings emissions legislation. In the next few years, regulations will be drafted specifying the mechanics and requirements for compliance, a new city office will be charged with implementation at the Department of Buildings, an advisory council will review the options for a carbon tax or carbon trading, and key city energy, business, and buildings organizations are stepping up to offer guidance and training while the financing tools are put in place.

Factors for success (and their limits)

OneNYC, both as an overall sustainability planning process in 2015 and in one of its key climate spinoff efforts on buildings, relied on several strategies:

1 Systems thinking

The OneNYC team approached the issue of planning for long-term sustainability as a system, with interconnected and interrelated forces and dynamics at play. This led to an expansion of agencies that were included in the overall planning process as well as the inclusion of 50 key stakeholders in the BTWG. The advantage of casting such a wide net was that the city could better identify previously unknown dynamics and information, including on data conflicts and ongoing efforts, before final decisions were made. The disadvantage was that the policy-planning process was much more complicated, and at times it was difficult to assess which factors were the most relevant. However, the factors that were the most appropriate tended to rise to the surface as the process went on.

2 Inclusion

The city looked for information from a wide variety of sources, both internally and externally. Being aware of the UN's SDG process enriched the OneNYC discussions and meant that the plan could serve as a roadmap for cities and others in the future, as it also contributed to the UN's understanding of how goals could be implemented on the ground. At the same time, inviting input from local elected officials, stakeholders, and city residents raised unforeseen facts about how draft visions and policies might succeed or fail. The additional input also introduced other ideas to consider.

This was true of the BTWG effort, as well. Although casting a wide net in that case was not enough to achieve unanimity among the participants, it served to narrow the issues and identify common ground, including on data. In many cases, participants were surprised to find themselves agreeing more than disagreeing. Bringing together technical experts with those who would be most affected, whether they agreed with each other or not, was one way that New York City was able to devise a path forward on complicated and controversial issues. This helped create a shared language, culture, and set of values, at least among those who were developing OneNYC and the building emissions strategy.

3 Importance of data

New York City, with its traditional orientation toward finance, insurance, and real estate, which remain its largest economic sectors, has a culture of valuing numbers and data. This culture served the OneNYC process well; it helped find a baseline of facts and described the current status of key indicators. The design process kept returning to the research and modeling, rather than relying on assumptions and conclusions. Qualitative as well as quantitative data were important. Moreover, studying the data and analyses revealed opportunities for better and more targeted policies. Data became the common language in many instances. In both OneNYC and the more technical BTWG, understanding the conditions at hand and modeling a number of scenarios for the future enabled City Hall and participants at least to reach a consensus on the definition of the problem. In addition, these data allowed the city to develop indicators and metrics by which to measure progress annually.

4 Design thinking

Participants were presented with and developed multiple drafts. The process was a circular one, seeking additional ideas and data until the deadlines approached. This was unlike past policymaking efforts and took some adjustment. The key was sending the clear signal that creative ideas were valued and proposing them during the design process would have no negative consequences. Ideas were invited, without cynicism or premature judgment; they were tested, data was tested, assumptions were revised, and new ideas and data were then developed and tested again, with the process repeating itself a number of times. This method invited a spirit of collaboration, rather than a contest of wills. The emphasis on data also aided the process.

5 Identification of common values

As the data were being analyzed and revised, the city's teams were also teasing out the answer to the question: "To what end?" If the goal was to set up a framework for New York's long-term sustainability, or thriving, then an agreement outlining what that meant had to be made.

For the de Blasio administration, in developing OneNYC those values sprang from the principles espoused in the mayoral race and later in the interagency working groups, as refined or modified by input and challenges from advisory board members, local elected officials, stakeholders, and city residents. In the case of the BTWG, while there was broad agreement that climate change was real and New York was vulnerable, not everyone shared the view that the timeline for changes was realistic or even the best way forward. In the end, it took multiple processes and negotiations—through a period of years—along with political will from the legislative branch, to enact the regulations that would move the goals ahead. While the BTWG may have largely agreed on the data, it was not enough in and of itself to move the buildings-emissions goals forward at that time. However, the data and the collaborative working relationships established in the BTWG did contribute to the final bill in 2019 and will continue to inform the rulemakings and programs that unroll from the bill in the next few years.

Conclusion

New York City's steps toward collaboration in climate and sustainability planning are far from complete. In the years to come, agency officials, the city council, and the local community will continue to grapple with the difficult questions of affordability, inclusion, and climate action. The sustainability-planning process in New York as well as in other cities will continue to evolve as conditions change, programs are evaluated, and new data is found. OneNYC laid a foundation that launched a new direction for the city and served as a model for other cities, and it will continue to do so.

References

Brundtland Commission. *Our Common Future*. Oxford: Oxford University Press, 1987.
City of New York. *New York City Charter: As Amended Through July 2004*, Chapter 1, sec. 20, 2004, www.nyc.gov/html/records/pdf/section%201133_citycharter.pdf.
———. *PlaNYC: A Greener, Greater New York*, 2007, www.nyc.gov/html/planyc/downloads/pdf/publications/full_report_2007.pdf.
———. *One New York: The Plan for a Strong and Just City*, 2015, Accessed December 9, 2019, www.nyc.gov/html/onenyc/downloads/pdf/publications/OneNYC.pdf.
———. *One City Built to Last: Technical Working Group Report*, 2016, https://www1.nyc.gov/html/gbee/downloads/pdf/TWGreport_04212016.pdf.
Martin, Roger. *The Design of Business*. Boston: Harvard Business Press, 2009.
Meadows, Donella H. *Thinking in Systems: A Primer*, White River Junction, VT: Chelsea Green Publishing, 2008.
New York City Council. *Climate Mobilization Act*, n.d., https://council.nyc.gov/data/green/.

United Nations. *Sustainable Development Goals*, n.d., accessed July 3, 2019, https://sustainabledevelopment.un.org/?menu=1300.

Walker, Hunter. "Bill de Blasio Tells 'A Tale of Two Cities' at His Mayoral Campaign Kickoff." *Observer*, January 27, 2013, https://observer.com/2013/01/bill-de-blasio-tells-a-tale-of-two-cities-at-his-mayoral-campaign-kickoff/.

Chapter 2

Communities

Teaming up with companies, cities, states, academia (The RAFT)

Elizabeth Andrews, Tanya Denckla Cobb,
Michelle Covi, and Angela M. King

The Resilience Adaptation Feasibility Tool

The question hung in the air, unanswered. More than a dozen academics and representatives of coastal localities had gathered in March 2015 at William & Mary Law School to pool knowledge and brainstorm next steps to help Virginia's coastal localities become more resilient to rising seas and recurrent flooding. Participants shared accomplishments over the last five years and what was underway now. Casting into the future for new ideas and next steps had not yet netted any big fish. Most people had left to return to their disparate communities, only a few diehards remained, and now a more focused question had been posed: "What could incentivize, catalyze, or motivate localities to make meaningful change on the ground, now?" Formulating the right question is often the most difficult part of any endeavor. At this small brainstorming meeting, local government (or "locality" as defined by Virginia code to mean a county, city, or town) representatives explained that academic studies and climate models were informative for building understanding but did not catalyze change. Coastal localities were unable to use studies and models to take meaningful action to become more resilient, not for lack of interest but because elected officials could not connect longitudinal studies and models with simple steps that could be taken during their short-term planning horizons while in office.

The reformulated question was fundamentally different and yielded an unexpected answer: *a report card*. A coastal resilience report card could galvanize residents to lobby their elected representatives for resilience measures and trigger competition with other localities, thereby catalyzing localities to take meaningful action. But the idea also contained many potential pitfalls. Would a report card be welcomed, resisted, or seen as punitive? If a locality wanted to improve its coastal resilience "grade" but didn't have the resources to act, would a coastal resilience report card be viewed as just one more unwelcome, unfunded burden? Or might a locality's politics dismiss the importance of coastal resilience? With these doubts and questions in mind, it would take what would eventually become a three-university academic partnership

DOI: 10.4324/9780429281242-3

another year of research and discussion with localities and advisers before The RAFT's three-part process took shape.

The context for The RAFT

Coastal Virginia is particularly vulnerable to flooding because it is experiencing the fastest rate of sea level rise on the East Coast of the United States (Ezer and Atkinson, 2015). In addition to global sea level rise due to climate change, the region has significant ground subsidence (Boon, Brubaker, and Forrest, 2010) and has experienced the effects of changes to the Gulf Stream that produce a "hotspot" of sea level rise extending northward from Cape Hatteras (Ezer and Atkinson, 2014). Interactions among ocean currents, sea level, and storms can produce disproportionate effects during relatively small storms (Ezer, 2018). Storm events are also becoming more extreme (Smirnov et al., 2017). They are overwhelming stormwater infrastructure and causing frequent floods, with roads and low-lying communities being particularly vulnerable (Virginia Institute of Marine Science, 2013).

In addition to the physical vulnerability, the governance structure within coastal Virginia has made it difficult to be more resilient as a region. The demographics of Virginia's coastal region are richly variegated: from scarcely populated rural areas to dense urban settings, extreme poverty to wealth, and tiny towns with as few as 200 people to the state's largest city, Virginia Beach, which has nearly 500,000 inhabitants. Similarly, the economies vary widely, from single-industry economies such as Tangier Island's blue crab-based fishery to broadly diversified economies that include military bases, tourism, busy ports, technology firms, and farming.

The urban area of the coast is Hampton Roads, made up of 17 different localities representing 1.7 million residents, many of which are taking measures to become resilient to coastal hazards independently from their neighbors. Cities in Hampton Roads, such as Norfolk and Virginia Beach, have been national leaders in planning for coastal resilience. For example, Norfolk participated in the Rockefeller 100 Resilient Cities program starting in 2014, and the regional Dutch Dialogues in 2015 focused on neighborhoods in the cities of Norfolk and Hampton. However, coastal rural areas are often left behind because their funding and staff resources are stretched to take care of immediate concerns, such as schools, and much of their infrastructure is maintained by the state. While regional planning district commissions can assist with these coastal locality needs, in theory, their responsibilities are limited by state law and by the need to have agreement from all member localities. Additionally, each locality depends on property taxes to fund its government services, and because many of the most threatened properties are expensive waterfront homes, there is a tendency for the locality to deny, or at least not openly discuss, the threat to the community that might result from lost tax revenue as residents abandon flooding coastal properties.

University researchers and environmental groups have recognized the threat of sea level rise to Virginia's wetlands since at least 2005. Since 2010, entities such as the Hampton Roads Planning District Commission have studied the impact of sea level rise on regional infrastructure. Since 2012, a growing body of reports by a broad array of coastal experts—including the US Army Corps of Engineers, CoreLogic (a leading data analytics firm), contractors for the City of Norfolk and City of Virginia Beach, the Virginia Institute of Marine Science, and other university researchers—has described the substantial risk to the region from sea level rise and associated flooding and explored potential solutions.

Early engagement efforts were funded by Virginia Sea Grant, a national network of 33 university-based programs established by the National Oceanic and Atmospheric Administration (NOAA), to support a healthy coastal environment and economy. Engagement efforts included listening sessions in Virginia Beach facilitated by the University of Virginia (UVA) Institute for Environmental Negotiation (IEN) in 2010–11, and the Old Dominion University-facilitated Hampton Roads Sea Level Rise/Flooding Adaptation Forum in 2012, which has continued meeting quarterly ever since.

The military, which makes up 40 percent of the gross domestic product in the Hampton Roads region, has been very actively planning for sea level rise on their bases. Traditionally, the federal government does not get involved in local affairs. However, in light of the severe threat that sea level rise poses to national security and military readiness in coastal regions, the military has begun partnering with Virginia's local governments in the urbanized Hampton Roads area, where it has an extensive presence with 39 installations and sites. Over the last decade, more than a dozen initiatives have engaged different sectors of Virginia's coastal region, including the military. In fact, one such recent initiative has been a Joint Land Use Study (JLUS) funded by the US Navy in partnership with the Hampton Roads Planning District Commission. The military's engagement with community planning, however, still has significant barriers, including the need for congressional approval and appropriation for cost-incurring military activities. To address these barriers, in 2014 Old Dominion University led a "whole of government" effort, the Intergovernmental Pilot Project, centered on engagement across both the military and the community to plan regionally for sea level rise (Yusuf et al., 2018).

Despite these efforts to advance resilience across coastal Virginia, many communities, particularly rural coastal areas, have been left behind. There has not been a state-wide comprehensive effort to engage all vulnerable coastal communities in resilience efforts at the local level, so The RAFT took on this challenge to provide a means of catalyzing localities to act. To date, The RAFT has focused on working with towns and counties in rural areas, as they have fewer resources than urban areas to address their resilience. Though the military does not have a real presence in these rural coastal communities, when The

RAFT begins working in the highly urbanized Hampton Roads region, the military will be invited to participate in The RAFT process.

Developing and testing The RAFT

A multi-university, interdisciplinary academic partnership initiated The RAFT in 2015 to create an assessment and response decision framework that would assist coastal communities in evaluating risks to coastal flooding, prioritizing action to increase resilience, and identifying sources of technical assistance and funding. The success of this partnership—initiated by IEN with the Virginia Coastal Policy Center (VCPC) at William & Mary Law School and Old Dominion University (ODU)/the Virginia Sea Grant Climate Adaptation Resilience Program (the "Collaborative Team")—reflects the strong commitment of each partner to help Virginia coastal localities increase their resilience.

Representatives from state and local government, nonprofit organizations, and academic institutions have also supported this effort to move beyond academic studies and climate models by serving on The RAFT Advisory Committee and focus groups. Additionally, local and regional government staff have represented the interests of residents and industries in the area, including the military. This support first began with the March 2015 meeting of more than a dozen academics and representatives of coastal localities at William & Mary Law School described at the start of this chapter, pooling knowledge and brainstorming next steps to help Virginia's coastal localities become more resilient to rising seas, flooding, and other coastal hazards.

The Collaborative Team discussed the possible roles for the Advisory Committee and decided that, in the absence of funding, it would be hard to ask its members to do more than provide feedback on the Scorecard and The RAFT process. From spring 2016 through winter 2018, the more than 20-member Advisory Committee provided ongoing guidance and feedback to the Collaborative Team concerning the selection of pilot communities for development of the Scorecard and an initial launch of The RAFT in the spring of 2017.

Additionally, the Collaborative Team convened two focus groups: one composed of 14 state and local government representatives to evaluate whether the Scorecard relied on objective indicators and covered relevant issue areas; and another composed of ten academics and community representatives to consider whether the Scorecard adequately addressed social equity (see Figure 2.1 for an overview of the advisory groups).

With a focus on community-level action, the localities themselves played a crucial role in The RAFT. The Collaborative Team decided that for resilience efforts to be sustainable, they needed to engage directly with local government. Local government staff, who were knowledgeable about resilience and engaged in local measures to improve resilience, provided input and support by serving on the Advisory Committee and focus groups. Localities needing support in

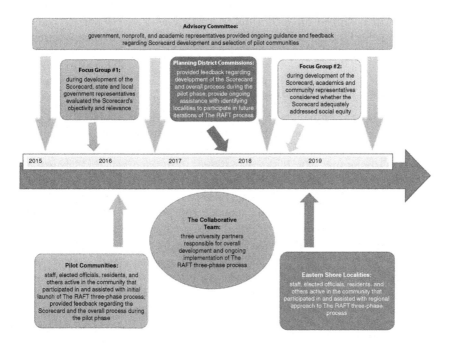

Figure 2.1 The RAFT: Project advisors
Source: the author

developing or implementing resilience initiatives were selected to engage with
The RAFT process.

Basics of The RAFT

The fundamental approach of the Collaborative Team was that resilience action
had to be tailored to the needs of the community by the community itself. In its
2017–18 pilot process, as described below, the Collaborative Team worked with
a city, a county, and a town, each with different needs and cultures. As a result of
the success of the pilot and feedback from the communities that the process was
valued, in 2018–19, the Collaborative Team worked with towns and counties
on the Eastern Shore of Virginia, using a regional approach while maintaining
the individual community-led focus for development and implementation of
each locality's Resilience Action Checklist.

The process

The RAFT process is not just a report of a locality's score without additional
interaction or support, as with many other assessment tools. Instead, the scoring

is followed by a community workshop to develop a Resilience Action Checklist, and then it is capped off with a full year of Collaborative Team assistance in achieving checklist items. These three phases are intended to move communities to meaningful action quickly:

Phase One: The RAFT Scorecard

Unlike existing assessment tools and scorecards, The RAFT Scorecard measures a locality's economic and social resilience in addition to its environmental resilience. The Scorecard is divided into five categories: (1) Policy, Leadership, and Collaboration; (2) Risk Assessment and Emergency Management; (3) Infrastructure Resilience; (4) Planning for Resilience; and (5) Community Engagement, Health, and Well-Being. Each of these categories has five sections worth four points, for an overall total of 100 points. Over the course of a few months, graduate students utilize the comprehensive Scorecard to conduct assessments of selected localities. The first step in these assessments involves online research to locate local codes, plans, and reports, as well as information from other sources such as nonprofit organizations, academic institutions, or regional organizations that are active in the locality. The second step involves conversations with local staff to clarify remaining questions or identify additional sources of information.

Phase Two: Resilience Action Checklist

Scorecard results are presented to the locality at a workshop of community leaders—which may include local government staff, local elected officials, business owners, residents, and representatives of state agencies and non-profit organizations—to review the locality's strengths and opportunities for improving resilience. The Collaborative Team facilitates this workshop, where community leaders prioritize their greatest opportunities for increasing local resilience and create one-year Resilience Action Checklists, which identify specific action items to help the locality achieve the goal.

Phase Three: Implementation

Crucially, The RAFT approach does not stop at either the assessment or the planning stage. To encourage successful implementation, the Collaborative Team provides support and assistance to the locality for one year. This support includes holding regular check-in calls to track progress with respect to the Resilience Action Checklist items and assisting with completion of items within the Collaborative Team's areas of expertise. For example, IEN may facilitate a meeting, ODU may develop communication materials, and VCPC may conduct legal research and analysis. The one-year time frame balances the need for sufficient time to implement identified action items with the importance of producing results quickly to increase local capacity and build teams that can carry on resilience action. Additionally, a defined one-year time frame for implementation assistance enables the Collaborative Team to allocate resources for the participation of additional localities in subsequent cycles of the RAFT process.

The pilot communities

To test this three-phase process in 2017, the Collaborative Team convened a meeting of its Advisory Committee to review the final Scorecard and the overall RAFT process, and make recommendations for the first three pilot communities. Ultimately, after exploratory conversations with the recommended localities, the Collaborative Team selected the city of Portsmouth, Gloucester County, and the town of Cape Charles, on the basis of several criteria, including a willingness to participate, physical vulnerability to coastal flooding, stage of comprehensive planning, and diversity of demographics, municipality type, density, and size. Additionally, the pilot communities represented three different regions of coastal Virginia. As each locality had different resources, staffing challenges, histories with flooding, and priorities, the Collaborative Team tailored its approach to these differences.

Creating a collaborative framework for The RAFT

Collaboration is challenging for a host of reasons, not the least of which are different perspectives, interests, skill sets, and participant personalities. But collaboration works well when time is taken at the outset to articulate values and highest aspirations along with the specific needs and behaviors that will enable achievement of these aspirations (Dukes, Stephens, and Piscolish, 2009). For The RAFT to succeed, each member of the Collaborative Team knew from extensive personal experience with localities that an effort to build coastal resilience could only work if the localities themselves were in the driver's seat. Therefore, a fundamental shared value guiding the Collaborative Team from the outset was that locality input should be a key component helping to steer the process. This meant engaging in extensive consultations from the start with those who understand Virginia's coastal peoples and places: discussing what approaches might work best, meeting localities where they are in the resilience process, and working with existing frameworks. Practically speaking, implementing this value has meant using The RAFT process to highlight the locality's strengths and opportunities for improving resilience, support the locality's chosen priorities for one-year actions, bolster connections between community leaders that enable joint work on resilience challenges, and be honest and transparent throughout about what The RAFT can and cannot do for the locality.

Supporting local agency also impacted how the Collaborative Team communicated and framed both the issues associated with increasing coastal hazards and community resilience. The Collaborative Team framed each community's risk and possible responses in ways that would be locally relevant, salient, and actionable. Flood risk was a major focusing theme for emergency communications and the need for communications improvements became apparent when these communities experienced storm-related flooding and evacuations. By focusing on issues relevant to the community and timescales in which a community can make a difference, the Collaborative Team practiced the principle of meeting the community where it was and then facilitated action to help it go where it needed to go to become more resilient.

The Collaborative Team's positive relationships with locality staff also affected the choice of language used. Collaborative Team members agreed that it was important for The RAFT to be supportive rather than punitive or judgmental; localities are struggling to do their best to deliver services with limited staff, resources, and authority. For this reason, the Collaborative Team decided to use the term "scorecard" rather than report card. In addition, when locality members of The RAFT Advisory Committee noted that staff members often think "plan" refers to a formally developed and adopted program, the Collaborative Team dropped it in favor of the more specific "checklist" to avoid apprehension and confusion.

Finding "higher (collaboration) ground" with The RAFT

Three key aspects of The RAFT distinguish it from other report card and assessment projects. The first distinguishing characteristic is that The RAFT represents a successful long-term collaboration between three universities. Most university collaborations coalesce around a narrow research question to test a hypothesis with specific research deliverables under a specific grant, after which the collaboration usually ends. In contrast, The RAFT is a collaboration involving the broad goal of advancing coastal resilience in multiple dimensions, over a long period of time, and requiring multiple sources of funding. Also notable is that while each member of the Collaborative Team brings different experiences, professional networks, and skills, all are oriented within their respective fields toward community engagement and improving community resilience. In addition to this core internal collaboration among the three universities, circles of collaboration extend outward from the core Collaborative Team to the Advisory Committee, the focus groups, state government agencies, and the staff and citizens of the localities being scored, all of whom are participating either as part of their job or, for citizen leaders, as volunteers.

The method of collaboration among faculty, staff, and students at the three university centers has also been a key to success. Others have noted the remarkable nature of this partnership, since academic institutions too often can be siloed in their efforts and because collaborations often fail for lack of institutional incentives or support for collaboration, difficulty communicating and working effectively across disciplines, and academic demands for giving primacy to individual researchers' own work. The Collaborative Team overcame these challenges by holding weekly conference calls, exploring resources that could be tapped at each of the universities, and brainstorming as the project evolved. This process has afforded an important and hoped-for result: it has built trust between the partners. The distinct subject-matter expertise of all three programs—Planning and Community Engagement at UVA, Law and Policy at William & Mary, and Science and Communications at ODU—means Collaborative Team members complement one another, bring different valuable experiences and perspectives to the project, and provide a well-rounded approach to the challenges faced by coastal communities. Collaborative Team members have learned to trust one another's ability to step in and answer questions according to their expertise, discern potential problems or challenges, and provide high quality, timely materials in support of The RAFT effort. That all three universities are public also has been helpful, since all partners face the same grant-processing requirements and share a similar commitment to assist local governments in the Commonwealth.

A second distinguishing characteristic of The RAFT is that it offers more than just a report card grade of a community's resilience efforts. Most other sustainability or resilience report cards or scorecards that the Collaborative Team reviewed consisted of locality *self*-scoring, with a primary focus on current on-the-ground environmental, economic, or resilience conditions. Scoring tended to use subjective metrics, meaning that results could vary widely, depending on who did the scoring. (An example of a subjective metric might be: "How often does the community do XYZ?"; with possible answers being "Very often, Often, Unsure, Not often, Never.") By contrast, The RAFT provides a comprehensive assessment of all three elements of community resilience (environmental, economic, and social), including consideration of social equity throughout. The assessment is not self-scored but conducted *independently* by the three universities. Further, the Scorecard metrics are *objective,* meaning each question is formulated to be answerable with a simple yes/no, which in turn means the assessment scores should be *replicable* and consistent regardless of who does the scoring. Finally, the focus of The RAFT Scorecard assessment is on planning and programmatic opportunities rather than current on-the-ground conditions or individual projects, enabling localities to take a long-term proactive view of their resilience efforts.

The third element distinguishing The RAFT from other tools is its *full-service* nature. Most or all other sustainability or resilience scorecards are a finite, self-contained activity, meaning that once the assessment is conducted and the score received, the locality is left to figure out what to do to improve its score. During IEN's early research phase, students interviewed other scorecard developers and recipients and learned that, while the scorecard provided important insights and information, localities found it hard to make changes based on the scorecard findings. With this insight, the Collaborative Team designed The RAFT to assist localities in moving beyond the Scorecard assessment (Phase 1) into action. The Collaborative Team–facilitated RAFT workshop (Phase 2) creates a space for community leaders to discuss their needs and develop a one-year Resilience Action Checklist. Following the workshop, the collaboration continues to support the locality (Phase 3) through implementation of its one-year Resilience Action Checklist. Unlike other scorecards, in this model The RAFT uses its Scorecard as a diagnostic springboard, not a prescriptive tool, for discussion. This means community participants are free to decide on priorities for the Checklist that may or may not derive directly from the Scorecard findings but may instead draw on local knowledge of what would make a difference and be achievable within the year. The benefit of this three-part process is that The RAFT brings local leaders together to discuss resilience with one another, often for the first time, and normalizes discussion of resilience beyond the physical impacts of flooding and coastal hazards. Rather than forcing solutions on a community or leaving them with no solutions at all, The RAFT prioritizes local knowledge and decision-making in the creation of its Resilience Action Checklist (see Figure 2.2 for an example of the Checklist).

The RAFT process supports community-driven resilience that is more actionable and sustainable over time. Similarly, the process creates local "Implementation Teams" of locality staff and community leaders, which help localities build their capacity for continuing meaningful action into the future. All of these strategies together contribute to The RAFT's success, which hinges on the simple concept of opening communication pathways that did not previously exist and that will continue as a legacy of The RAFT.

Some lessons learned

For The RAFT to support greater resilience in Virginia's coastal localities, the Collaborative Team envisions many years of continuing to adapt the tool to evolving needs. Yet, even at this early stage, some insights are possible.

First, The RAFT three-phase process has shown that it provides localities an incentive to increase resilience. Like other report cards or scorecards that have raised awareness but failed to produce change, the Scorecard assessment alone would likely not catalyze change. For example, for the town of Cape Charles, it was an educational presentation to the Town Council, one of the locality's Resilience Action Checklist items, that proved to be a turning point in a broader conversation about resilience. It enabled town staff to initiate development of the town's first Resilience Plan. For the town of Saxis, the workshop discussion of Scorecard findings enabled the town's Implementation Team several weeks later to develop specific actions that would immediately help the town identify and communicate with its vulnerable populations to prepare for Florence, an imminent hurricane. For Northampton County, a work session with the planning commission enabled commissioners to identify ways to incorporate resilience planning into the county's new Comprehensive Plan. These are just

ONANCOCK RESILIENCE ACTION CHECKLIST

PRODUCT OF THE RAFT RESILIENCE ACTION WORKSHOP AUGUST 2018

1. COMPLETE COMPREHENSIVE PLAN

- Work with Town Manager to finish developing the Town's Comprehensive Plan.

2. DESIGN RESILIENT WHARF WATERFRONT

- The Wharf needs repairs to the bulkhead and boat ramp, and drainage could be improved to prevent flooding of parking lot. Additionally, the historic Hopkins Building needs repairs to waterfront.

3. PROJECTED ECONOMIC IMPACT ANALYSIS

- Investigate how investments in resiliency now will promote economic development in the future.

4. COMMUNITY EDUCATION AND OUTREACH

- Provide information to the community about resiliency, promoting continuity between Council decisions and Town resilience.

Figure 2.2 Example of a resilience checklist
Source: University of Virginia

a few examples of the many advances that localities have made through The RAFT process to increase their resilience. While none of the individual pieces of The RAFT process may be novel, connecting them into a 16-month process elevates community attention to resilience, supports local agency and implementation, and transforms the parts into a holistic agent of change.

Second, in terms of how the Scorecard assessment would be perceived, the Collaborative Team feared that its assessment would be seen as punitive, but that has not been realized. Other parts of The RAFT process have not always been welcome, however. Some localities do not want to focus on the long-term coastal hazard issue when they have more pressing short-term issues, such as funding a new school or health clinic. One locality with a population of less than 1,000, facing severe erosion and land loss from sea level rise and coastal storms, wondered how a priority action list focusing on policies could help its immediate shoring-up needs or how implementation would even be possible with so few human resources. The RAFT Collaborative Team adapted the process to that community's different needs by bringing together experts to focus on a specific erosion-related problem rather than working on a comprehensive resilience checklist like the ones other localities had developed.

Still, whether localities are small with few resources, facing severe erosion and coastal hazards, or economically stressed, most have welcomed the RAFT process and expressed gratitude for the resources the universities bring to bear on their resilience. It has been affirming to the Collaborative Team and its advisors that, even in this politically divisive time, a focus on resilience and immediate needs within the community makes it possible to avoid divisive political views about climate change. This was achieved not by focusing on climate change per se, but rather by framing resilience around the daily experiences of the local residents, who are seeing a significant on-the-ground increase in damage from flooding and coastal hazards, as well as the impacts of those risks on their everyday quality of life. Rural coastal Virginia is challenged by both sea level rise and economic disparities. Processes that can highlight these needs—and bring solutions that can address community viability in both areas—are welcomed.

Over the past year, the Collaborative Team has learned to be flexible in adapting and administering The RAFT assessment. For example, the Team was asked by members of its Advisory Committee to conduct the assessment on a regional scale to accelerate the timetable for assisting all Virginia coastal localities as quickly as possible and to see if regional synergies and efficiencies might be found in the implementation phase. The regional approach turned out to offer a superior method. As customization of individual locality needs and implementation continued, so did the participative nature of the process. Now, the localities were also able to learn from each other at the first workshops, and tools developed for one locality could be shared with other interested localities. Examples of these shared tools were emergency preparedness refrigerator magnets and detailed maps showing different elements of risk. In agreeing to shift its model to a regional approach, after gaining support from the region's planning district commission to work with seven Eastern Shore localities (including the counties of Accomack and Northampton and the towns of Chincoteague, Onancock, Saxis, Tangier, and Wachapreague), the Collaborative Team realized it could also play an important role in helping identify shared regional needs that could be brought to the state government's attention. For example, on the Eastern Shore, the Virginia Coastal Policy Center conducted a regional meeting with the Virginia Department of Transportation and The RAFT implementation teams to address identified needs in each of the counties and towns. This meeting not only served to connect localities with their regional representatives in the state government, but also helped them understand how the region can work better together and elevate their transportation concerns to the state level.

A final lesson learned is that a key to The RAFT's success is evolving and expanding partnership circles with academia, NGOs, the private sector (including local businesses as well as environmental and engineering consulting firms), and government. Unforeseen at the start, the need to leverage expertise beyond the Collaborative Team became clear during work with the three pilot communities. For example, the town of Cape Charles hoped for an assessment of its green infrastructure, which was beyond the scope of what the team could provide. Assistance was sought from a faculty colleague, who agreed to focus her next graduate planning class on developing a green infrastructure assessment for the town. Rather than trying to do it all, and thereby engaging in classic organizational "turf protection," the circle of work was expanded with numerous other partners. As a result of The RAFT, new mapping tools were completed by reaching out to other UVA faculty and colleagues at a nonprofit organization; a community survey on emergency communication was developed in partnership with a planning district commission and distributed to local government staff for completion; and the need for a solution to address a flooding waterfront area led to a private engineering firm providing pro bono assistance through the Virginia Sea Grant resilience fellowship program. By working with The RAFT, localities are able to access the Collaborative Team's contacts in academia, NGOs, the private sector, and government, and thereby greatly expand their skill sets for building coastal resilience.

The RAFT concept and its tools and products are available as free and openly available resources through the project website (https://raft.ien.virginia.edu). Conference presentations, invitational talks, and individual connections and networks are all ways in which the Collaborative Team is sharing these tools and lessons with other states.

Grounded in a pragmatic approach that focuses on community-wide resilience to coastal hazards and avoids politically charged language, coupled with values that support locality leadership, agency, and an expanding network to support future resilience efforts, the Collaborative Team believes The RAFT is poised to play a key role in supporting Virginia's coastal resilience over the long term.

References

Boon, John D., John M. Brubaker, and David R. Forrest. *Chesapeake Bay Land Subsidence and Sea Level Change: An Evaluation of Past and Present Trends and Future Outlook.* A Report to the US Army Corps of Engineers, Norfolk District, 2010, https://doi.org/10.21220/V58X4P.

Dukes, E. Franklin, John B. Stephens, and Marina A. Piscolish. *Reaching for Higher Ground: Creating Purpose-Driven, Principled, and Powerful Groups.* Charleston, SC: BookSurge, 2009.

Ezer, Tal, and Larry P. Atkinson. "Accelerated Flooding Along the US East Coast: On the Impact of Sea-Level Rise, Tides, Storms, the Gulf Stream, and the North Atlantic Oscillations." *Earth's Future*, 2, no. 8 (2014): 362–82, https://doi.org/10.1002/2014EF000252.

Ezer, Tal, and Larry P. Atkinson. "Sea Level Rise in Virginia–Causes, Effects and Response." *Virginia Journal of Science* 66, no. 3 (2015): 355–69.

Ezer, Tal. "The Increased Risk of Flooding in Hampton Roads: On the Roles of Sea Level Rise, Storm Surges, Hurricanes, and the Gulf Stream." *Marine Technology Society Journal* 52, no. 2 (2018): 34–44.

Smirnov, Dmitry, John Giovannettone, Brian Batten, Greg Johnson, and Shanda Davenport. "Assessing Historical and Projected Trends in Heavy Rainfall in the Virginia Beach Area." *Modeling and Managing Extreme Precipitation*, May 19, 2017, https://pdfs.semanticscholar.org/595f/c9472a936299eb53885f57258178c9593c90.pdf.

Virginia Institute of Marine Science. *Recurrent Flooding Study for Tidewater Virginia, SJR 76, 2012*, Report to the Governor and General Assembly of Virginia, Senate Document No. 3, Commonwealth of Virginia, Richmond, 2013, https://rga.lis.virginia.gov/Published/2013/SD3/PDF.

Yusuf, Juita-Elena Wie, Michelle Covi, Carol Considine, Burton St. John, Meagan Jordan, and J. Gail Nicula. "Toward a Whole-of-Government and Whole-of-Community Approach for Regional Adaptation to Sea Level Rise: Lessons Learned from the Hampton Roads Intergovernmental Pilot Project." In Chelsea Schelly and Aparajita Banerjee (Eds), *Environmental Policy and the Pursuit of Sustainability*. Abingdon and New York: Routledge, 2018: 63–78.

Chapter 3

Climate change and national security

Opportunities for learning and cooperation

Mark R. Read

Introduction

> When I look at climate change, it's in the category of sources of conflict around the world and things we have to respond to. So it can be great devastation requiring humanitarian assistance/disaster relief, which the US military certainly conducts routinely. In fact, I can't think of a year since I've been on active duty that we haven't conducted at least one operation in the Pacific along those lines due to extreme weather in the Pacific. And then, when you look at sources of conflict—shortages of water, and those kind of things—those are all sources of conflict. So, it is very much something that we take into account in our planning as we anticipate when, where, and how we may be engaged in the future and what capabilities we should have.
>
> (General Joe Dunford, Chairman of the
> Joint Chiefs of Staff, 2018)[1]

For many years, the US Department of Defense (DoD) has examined the relationship between climate change and national security, seeking to understand how climate change will affect national security interests domestically and internationally. The focus has changed over the past two decades as our collective understanding of the science of climate change has improved. The DoD, often in partnership with other government agencies, academia, or non-government organizations, has studied the effects of climate change on the mission of national security, its influence on defense infrastructure, and potential impact on personnel and equipment. The 2008 National Defense Authorization Act (NDAA) directed the executive branch, specifically the intelligence community and DoD, to conduct periodic assessments of climate change on national security. The NDAA is the federal law that specifies the annual budget and expenditures of the DoD, and the 2008 NDAA was the first to direct DoD action on climate change. Specifically, the Act directs that the next National

DOI: 10.4324/9780429281242-4

Security Strategy and National Defense Strategy shall include the following guidance for military planners:

> assess the risks of projected climate change to current and future missions of the armed forces, update defense plans based on these assessments, including working with allies and partners to incorporate climate mitigation strategies, capacity building, and relevant research and development, and develop the capabilities needed to reduce future impacts.
>
> (NDAA, 2008)

The NDAA also directs the next Quadrennial Defense Review to "examine the capabilities of the armed forces to respond to the consequences of climate change, in particular, preparedness for natural disasters from extreme weather events and other missions the armed forces may be asked to support" (ibid.). Finally, the NDAA directs the Secretary of Defense to use the mid-range consensus climate projections from the most recent assessment report of the Intergovernmental Panel on Climate Change. Following this directive, the ensuing National Security Strategies and Quadrennial Defense Reviews did indeed address the security implications of climate change.

More recently, the 2018 NDAA, passed by Congress and signed into law by the president, identifies that climate change is "a direct threat to the national security of the United States and is impacting stability in areas of the world both where the US Armed Forces are operating today, and where strategic implications for future conflict exist" (H.R.2810, 2018), and directs the Secretary of Defense to report on vulnerabilities to military installations and combatant commander requirements resulting from climate change over the next 20 years.[2] In 2019, a report by the US Government Accountability Office (GAO) determined that DoD installations "have not consistently assessed risks from extreme weather and climate change effects or consistently used projections to anticipate future climate conditions" (US Government Accountability Office, 2019). The GAO recommends that the DoD improve the climate resilience of installations and incorporate climate projections into installation master planning and facilities design. The US Army has included climate change as a theme of interest in its 2018–20 Key Strategic Issues List, seeking research to identify the potential impact of climate change on US national interests, emerging security challenges, and soldier readiness (Army War College, 2018).

While climate change presents challenges to national security, it also presents opportunities for cooperation and collaboration at several scales. In this chapter, I provide three brief examples of the national security community planning for climate change, including examples of cooperation. The first example takes place at the national and international level and involves the US Navy's response to climate change in the Arctic. The second example is set at a regional level, highlighting the challenges faced by the DoD as the armed forces cope with sea level rise in the Hampton Roads region of the Chesapeake Bay. The third example discusses how climate change is incorporated into the curriculum at the US Military Academy at West Point, preparing future officers at an individual level to cope with the complexities of the world in which they will lead soldiers following their graduation and commissioning.

Responding to a changing environment: Task Force Climate Change

The Arctic region is warming more rapidly than other regions of the planet, with a wide range of impacts including increased melting of ice sheets and reduced sea ice thickness and coverage (Osborne, Richter-Menge, and Jeffries, 2018). In 2009, the Chief of Naval Operations (the senior officer in the US Navy) formed the Navy's Task Force Climate Change (TFCC) to examine the implications of climate change for national security, specifically in the realm of naval operations, with a focus on a changing Arctic. Using a science-based approach, TFCC developed recommendations, plans, and actions to help the Navy adapt to and prepare for climate change impacts.

For decades, naval operations in the Arctic region have been limited primarily to submarines, operating below the Arctic sea ice, and aircraft. But decreasing sea ice in the Arctic means an increasing Navy role in surface operations and a change in the conditions for subsurface and air operations. The Navy saw the need to prepare for operations in a rapidly changing Arctic and created TFCC as part of its already-existing Office of the Oceanographer of the Navy. The Task Force had a mission and the authority to coordinate with other federal agencies and the academic community. The TFCC Charter spells out the background, guidance, and organization of the task force (Greenert, 2009). Made up of an Executive Steering Committee (ESC), the task force was directed by an admiral (the Oceanographer of the Navy), who reported directly to senior Navy leadership. The ESC included one- and two-star admiral (or equivalent) representatives from all major directorates on the Navy staff: US Fleet Forces Command, the Pacific Fleet, the US Coast Guard, and the National Atmospheric and Oceanic Administration (NOAA). Additionally, the task force included seven working groups, focusing on areas such as strategy, policy, missions and plans; installations and facilities; strategic communications and outreach; and environmental assessment and prediction. Each of the seven working groups had specific responsibilities. The task force focused first on the Arctic—the most pressing need for the Navy—and then other impacts of climate change.

From its outset, TFCC did not go it alone. Immediately, it partnered with NOAA and the US Coast Guard, quickly forged interagency partnerships within the DoD, and collaborated with other US government agencies and research centers (such as the National Aeronautics and Space Administration [NASA], US Geological Survey, Department of Homeland Security, National Center for Atmospheric Research, Oak Ridge National Lab, Los Alamos National Lab, and Department of the Interior), academic institutions, NGOs such as the Center for Naval Analyses [CNA] and the Consortium for Ocean Leadership), and international partners (including Canada, the United Kingdom, Norway, Finland, Sweden, Denmark, and Russia). The TFCC engaged more than 125 organizations. Each brought a unique background, perspective, or ability to the table. The collaboration took on many forms, including conferences, meetings, data sharing, networking, simulations, and participation in a series of naval exercises in the Arctic.[3] The TFCC also initiated a series of installation vulnerability assessments for Navy bases in the United States and overseas. Finally, the collaboration advanced US ability to predict the effects of climate change. This extensive cooperation was essential to completing the 2010 and 2014 *Roadmaps*, allowing TFCC to gather information to which it would not otherwise have had access, develop and analyze strategic courses of action for the Navy, and incorporate a wide range of perspectives on the future impact of climate change, both in the Arctic and globally.

Working with these partners and collaborators, TFCC sought to understand a range of climate change concerns. Near-term concerns included increasing Arctic maritime activity (due to decreased sea ice), partnership opportunities, and energy security initiatives (initiatives that reduce the Navy's carbon footprint). Mid- to long-term concerns included the impact of sea level rise on military installations and infrastructure, water resource challenges, and the potential increase in humanitarian assistance or disaster response operations caused or exacerbated by climate change. Finally, TFCC worked with its partners to study and plan through potential climate change "wild card" scenarios, including the impact of ocean acidification, abrupt climate change, and geoengineering. Each of the 125 partner organizations contributed to the efforts to varying degrees; some provided scientific data or analysis, while others cooperated throughout the Navy's collaborative efforts and continue to partner with the Navy in research, development, and planning. For example, CNA continues to publish reports related to climate change and security. Issued by its Military Advisory Board (a group of retired three- and four-star admirals and generals), its most recent report, *The Role of Water Stress in Instability and Conflict*, was published in late 2017 (CNA, 2017). And not all partners approached climate change from a national security perspective: many, especially the academic institutions, are involved from a purely academic perspective, interested in the science of climate change in the Arctic. Regardless, from the TFCC's outset, the Navy took a structured, deliberate approach to its collaboration, research, and planning efforts.

Perhaps the most important output of TFCC has been its *Roadmaps*. The first *Roadmap* was published in April 2010 (US Navy, 2010) and laid out a clear vision for TFCC and the Navy for the next four years. It outlined the Navy's approach to observing, predicting, and adapting to climate change and listed specific action items, objectives, and desired effects to be accomplished through three phases between 2010 and 2014. In 2014, TFCC published an updated *Roadmap*, the *US Navy Arctic Roadmap* (US Navy, 2014).

The *Arctic Roadmap* was more regionally focused than the 2010 *Roadmap*, but took a much longer, strategic perspective, charting a course out to 2030, with clear near-, mid-, and long-term objectives. The near- to mid-term object- ives focus on strengthening the Navy's operational capabilities in the region, improving expertise, and working with interagency and international part- ners. Long-term objectives, focused on 2030 and beyond, address possible requirements for an increasingly ice-free Arctic. The *2014 Roadmap* emphasized internal changes to the Navy's equipment, doctrine, and strategy for the Arctic and the importance of interagency and international cooperation in this com- plex, resource-rich, contested region, even highlighting opportunities for and examples of cooperation with a potential adversary, Russia.

In summary, TFCC provides a shining example of an organization within the US government identifying a complex problem, creating an organization to study the problem and then recommend solutions, providing resources for it to accomplish its mission, and codifying a strategy to help guide the organization and its partners into the future. The task force emphasized the need to "develop strong cooperative partnerships with interagency and international Arctic Region stakeholders" (US Navy, 2014: 19). Finally, TFCC recognized the need for, then created, a long-term strategy that considers a rapidly changing envir- onment, with a need to continuously re-examine changing conditions and make appropriate adjustments to the strategy. The Navy ended TFCC in March 2019 for reasons that are somewhat unclear. Nonetheless, TFCC remains an example for other organizations, both in and out of government, to learn from regarding adaptation to climate change and collaboration across institutional boundaries.

Challenges on the home front: sea level rise in the Hampton Roads region

One of the most significant challenges posed by a changing climate is sea level rise. The Hampton Roads region of the southern Chesapeake Bay is a series of low-lying peninsulas that are particularly susceptible to sea level rise. Many coastal areas in the region are also experiencing land subsidence and continuing development for commercial, residential, and government use, which can com- pound the effects of sea level rise. Recent decades have seen an increase in the frequency and intensity of coastal flooding events linked to storm surges, rain events, and high tides, and sea level rise in the region is accelerating. The region is experiencing the most significant sea level rise in the United States, with current projections of 2.3 to 5.2 feet by 2100. One study examined the number of hours per year that streets are flooded in a historic district in Norfolk, Virginia. The flooding frequency and duration has increased exponen- tially; currently streets in this area are flooded approximately 100 hours per year.

Another nearby area—a highly trafficked artery near Naval Station Norfolk—is projected to flood twice a day for an hour by 2040 (Atkinson, Ezer, and Smith, 2013). The area is home to more than 18 military installations, including Langley Air Force Base, three Army installations (Forts Eustis, Lee, and Story) and numerous marine and naval stations, including Naval Station Norfolk, the world's largest. In total, the bases are home to approximately 83,000 active-duty personnel, making up 5 percent of the region's 1.7 million inhabitants.

Rising sea levels and ground subsidence have resulted in increased flooding, which adversely affects existing infrastructure on the military bases, off-base residences of military families, and road networks used by civilian and military personnel who work at the installations. Sea level rise in the Hampton Roads area affects both military and civilian communities, and all communities must cooperate to find solutions to adapt. Clear, long-term solutions, to date, remain elusive, with no clear organization, agency, or person taking the lead, and no clear, unified plan moving forward.

The complexity of the local governments adds to the challenge of cooperation and leadership. Hampton Roads is a large area consisting of multiple local governments, state-level interests, and federal agencies. Currently, no comprehensive state- or regional-level plan addresses infrastructure vulnerability or sea level rise. The good news is that awareness of the issue is increasing, locally and nationally, and there is still time to take adaptive action; additionally, local-level comprehensive plans and regional-level hazard mitigation plans exist. Chapter 2 discusses one example of collaboration among communities, regional government, academia, and the private sector—the Resilience Adaptation Feasibility Tool (The RAFT)—but challenges remain among all stakeholders in the region.

The challenge faced by the DoD in the Hampton Roads region is indeed complex and, to date, does not present the same good news story as the TFCC. There is no clear assessment of the problem, no single agency or entity has been charged to take the lead on assessing and providing recommendations, and no roadmap has been created to chart the way forward, either for the military or the surrounding communities. Nonetheless, there is time to address this complex problem: although sea level rise is accelerating, and its effects are already being observed in the area, it is a relatively slow change. The Army Corps of Engineers has stated that 1.5 feet of sea level rise will be a tipping point for Naval Station Norfolk; this is expected to happen within the next 20 to 50 years. Many current and former members of the military, who have experience in this region, are working to raise awareness, identify community, state, and federal partners with whom to cooperate, and help develop near- and long-term solutions. In 2018, The Center for Climate and Security, a Washington, DC-based NGO focused on climate change and security issues, convened a panel of experts, including six high-ranking former military officers who made eight specific recommendations aimed at addressing the risk of sea level rise to US military installations and mission:

1) Identify and build capacity to address infrastructural, operational, and strategic risks
2) Integrate climate impact scenarios and projections into regular planning cycles
3) Make climate-related decisions that incorporate the spectrum of risk projections
4) Model catastrophic scenarios and incorporate them into planning and war gaming exercises
5) Work with international counterparts at key coastal bases abroad
6) Track trends in climate impacts as uncertainty levels are reduced
7) Maintain close collaboration with adjacent civilian communities
8) Invest in improvements in climate data and analysis.

Though not specifically focused on the Hampton Roads area, the majority of recommendations apply to that region (Femia, 2018: 6). While most of these recommendations have not been pursued yet, some recent, positive steps have been taken. One example is the Hampton Roads Sea Level Rise Preparedness and Resilience Intergovernmental Pilot Project, organized by Old Dominion University. This project brought together more than 75 local community leaders, military leaders, community planners, NGO representatives, scholars, and other stakeholders over a two-year period to develop a "whole of government mitigation and adaptation planning process and an integrated regional recommendation" (Steinhilber et al., 2016: 10).

The pilot project identified relevant conclusions, recommendations, and lessons. Among the many significant findings, it recommended that local stakeholders should maintain, institutionalize, and build relationships that facilitate ongoing collaboration. Institutionalization is especially important to offset personnel turnover. The project specifically recommended the creation of a standing regional authority focused on issues related to sea level rise to foster collaboration and planning. Additionally, it recommended better data integration and sharing among stakeholders.

Another recent, positive step that may bear fruit in the Hampton Roads region is the Defense Community Infrastructure Pilot Program (DCIP), a bipartisan effort included in the 2019 NDAA to make grants, cooperative agreements, and supplemental funds available to help state and local governments improve infrastructure near military installations (H.R.5515, 2019). The program requires state or local governments to contribute at least 30 percent of the funding for any infrastructure project, while the federal government would fund the balance. This cost-sharing is one way to ensure federal and local governments cooperate. The Hampton Roads region stands to benefit significantly from this cost-sharing pilot program: the US Army Corps of Engineers recently identified the city of Norfolk as one of nine high-risk areas on the East Coast with a large population and infrastructure vulnerable to coastal flooding. The economic analysis, based on a 15-inch sea level rise by 2075, estimates flood protection infrastructure costs of more than $1.5 billion for Norfolk (US Army Corps of Engineers, 2018). Although DCIP, currently authorized by Congress as a 10-year pilot program, may yield positive results for communities in the Hampton Roads, at the time of writing this program is less than a year old, so it is too early to tell what fruit this program may yield in this region or elsewhere.

Educating future leaders: climate change in the curriculum at West Point

Each year, the US Military Academy at West Point graduates and commissions approximately a third of the officers assessed into the US Army. Cadets at West Point undergo a rigorous four-year program that includes a top-tier undergraduate education. The academic coursework boasts a robust, 27-course liberal arts core curriculum, and each cadet selects an academic major (an additional 13 to 16 courses). All graduates earn a Bachelor of Science degree; approximately half of cadets choose a major in a STEM discipline, and half opt for a degree in the humanities or social sciences. Climate change and environmental stewardship are included in the curriculum in several ways. First, all cadets take a core physical geography course during their freshman or sophomore year. The course includes blocks on weather, climate, landforms, and culture, and includes a lesson specifically focused on climate change.

Climate is an important element of any basic geoscience curriculum and is also significant in the context of the study of warfare past, present, and future. As such, West Point has offered a course in climatology for decades and has included a climate block in the core physical geography course for a similar length of time. The core physical geography course, which spans 30 lessons, includes ten lessons focused on weather and climate, one of which is dedicated to climate change. The lesson on climate change was added to the course in 2004, because faculty realized it was an important, relevant topic and an increasing number of cadets wanted to understand the basics of climate science and climate change.

Additionally, several upper-level courses taken by cadets majoring in geography and environmental science include lessons or blocks of lessons on climate change. All environmental science majors (approximately 15 to 25 cadets each year for the past several years, out of a class of around 1,000) take a capstone course called Environmental Security, during which they study many aspects of climate change including its national security implications (domestically and internationally), the relationship between energy and climate change, and the Paris Agreement.

In addition to core and major courses, all cadets who do not major in engineering must take a Core Engineering Sequence (CES): a three-course sequence in one of six engineering disciplines, spanning three semesters. One of the six options is the Environmental Engineering Sequence, which focuses on current environmental issues and designing viable, sustainable solutions for them. The

Environmental Sequence is the most highly subscribed sequence, with 180 cadets in each year group signing up. It is also the most highly demanded sequence: interest has increased steadily over the past several years, with nearly twice as many cadets requesting the sequence (well over 300 in the past two years) as are able to take it (due to faculty and space limitations). The faculty includes several civilian and military scholars who have studied climate variability and change, and they continue to conduct research related to climate change. Cadets and faculty alike have opportunities to engage with the latest science and policy related to climate change through guest speakers, symposia, and conferences. Educating future Army officers about climate change remains an important part of preparing them to lead and serve in a complex, dangerous, and ever-changing world.

Conclusion

Climate change poses both immediate and long-term challenges for all of us, including those in the national security community. The DoD has turned to the best available climate science to understand the potential effects of a changing climate on its mission, at home and abroad. The three examples in this chapter provide a brief glimpse at different ways in which the DoD, in partnership with others, has studied and planned for a changing climate. The Navy's TFCC provides an excellent example of a federal agency identifying a challenge, creating a small, agile organization to study the challenge and then propose a flexible but robust strategy, working with a wide range of partners to prepare for climate change in the Arctic.

The challenges faced by the Navy and other military branches as sea level rises in the Hampton Roads region of Virginia demonstrate an ongoing problem with no clear solution, but it is a problem that the DoD acknowledges and stands ready to work with community partners to address. Stakeholders across the region have started to cooperate, negotiate, identify solutions, and find ways to fund and implement them, and recently the federal government has created new pathways of cooperation and cost-sharing to help.

Finally, the inclusion of climate change in the curriculum at West Point provides an example of an individual-level opportunity to educate future military leaders about one facet of the complex world in which they will soon be operating as leaders in the armed forces, preparing young men and women to "play in the sandbox" in the wide range of operating environments they will face.

Although different, each of these three examples provides important lessons. First, each example illustrates groups or organizations that take a long view of a complex problem, have identified possible solutions, and remain patient and persistent in working toward those solutions. Human nature often seeks quick wins and immediate results. Collaboration on climate change-related challenges is inherently complex and demands patience and persistence. Throughout its history, the US military has faced complex, long-term problems and applied its extensive strategic planning capability to clearly identify and work through such problems. Climate change represents yet another such long-term problem that the defense community is seeking to understand, prepare for, and adapt to.

Second, each example illustrates the critical importance of *leadership*: individuals or small groups determined to steer their organizations, and in many cases reach across boundaries to seek assistance and collaboration to identify and solve complex problems while seeking and capitalizing on opportunities as they emerge. In each of these cases, leaders often worked for years, guided by a mission or vision, to identify and define problems, pursue resources, and inspire others toward change. They quite often made mistakes along the way but learned from those mistakes. Although climate change has become politicized to some extent, military leaders remain apolitical, and view climate change not as a political issue but as a potential risk to mission, stability, infrastructure, and personnel.

Finally, each of the three examples in this chapter highlights ways in which the military cooperates with the scientific community. For most of the past century, partnerships between the defense and scientific communities have helped solve some of society's most challenging problems on issues ranging from human health and medicine to flight and space exploration. The defense community can often shift significant resources to focus research and development on problems that may not be a priority for the private sector. Collaboration around understanding, planning for, and adapting to climate change may be another such complex, long-term challenge.

Notes

1   Speech, November 5, 2018, Duke University Program in American Grand Strategy, https://www.youtube.com/watch?v=hKvpHtLs7sY&ab_channel=DukeUniversity DepartmentofPoliticalScience.
2   Combatant commanders are the four-star flag officers (general or admirals) responsible for one of the ten geographic or functional combatant commands, such as US European Command or US Special Operations Command.
3   The naval exercises in the Arctic include ICEX, a five-week, biennial exercise that includes a focus on understanding a changing Arctic environment and an emphasis on developing relationships with allies and partner organizations (US Navy, 2018).

References

Army War College. *Key Strategic Issues List, 2018–2020.* US Army War College Press, 2018.

Atkinson, Larry P., Tal Ezer, and Elizabeth Smith. "Sea Level Rise and Flooding Risk in Virginia." *Sea Grant Law and Policy Journal* 5, no. 2 (2018): 3–14.

Femia, Francesco. *Sea Level Rise and the US Military's Mission*, 2nd Edition. The Center for Climate and Security, 2018, https://climateandsecurity.org/militaryexpertpanel2018/.

Greenert, J. W. *Task Force Climate Change Charter*. Vice Chief of Naval Operations, Department of the Navy, 2009, http://navysustainability.dodlive.mil/files/2010/09/Task-Force-Climate-Change-Charter.pdf.

H.R.2810. *National Defense Authorization Act for Fiscal Year 2018*, Section 335, 2018.

H.R.5515. *National Defense Authorization Act for Fiscal Year 2019*, Section 2861, 2019.

NDAA. *National Defense Authorization Act for Fiscal Year 2008*. Public Law 110–181, Section 951, 2008.

Osborne, E., J. Richter-Menge, and M. Jeffries (Eds). *Arctic Report Card 2018*, 2018, https://www.arctic.noaa.gov/Report-Card.

Steinhilber, Emily E., Maura Boswell, Carol Considine, and Larry Mast. Hampton Roads Sea Level Rise Preparedness and Resilience Intergovernmental Pilot Project: Phase 2 Report, 2016, http://resilientvirginia.org/wp-content/uploads/2016/12/20161006-hampton-roads-phase-2-report.pdf.

US Army Corps of Engineers. *Norfolk Coast Storm Risk Management*, 2018, https://www.nao.usace.army.mil/NCSRM/.

US Government Accountability Office. "Climate Resilience: DoD Needs to Assess Risk and Provide Guidance on Use of Climate Projections in Installation Master Plans and Facilities Design." GAO-19–453, June 2019.

US Navy. *The US Navy Climate Change Roadmap*, 2010, https://www.hsdl.org/?abstract&did=8466#:~:text=The%20Navy%20'Climate%20Change%20Roadmap,fiscal%20year%5D10%2D14.

———. *The United States Navy Arctic Roadmap for 2014 to 2030*, 2014, http://navysustainability.dodlive.mil/files/2014/02/USN-Arctic-Roadmap-2014.pdf.

———. "ICEX 2018: Proving Ground for Submarine Arctic Operability and Warfighting," March 8, 2018, http://navylive.dodlive.mil/2018/03/08/icex2018/.

Chapter 4

Equity

Climate justice in Detroit

Kimberly Hill Knott

From the bottom up by force: because Detroit matters

Detroit, Michigan, has a rich and intriguing history. Detroit is commonly described as an innovation hub, from the launch of the automobile industry in 1903 to the launch of Motown in 1959. Many people migrated to the city because of the vast number of jobs and the opportunity to move into the middle class. Ford Motor Company became one of the first companies in the United States to establish a 40-hour work week, and it paid $5 per day to males—and later to females—more than doubling the amount of money an autoworker made in a day. This pay scale and other advances in manufacturing effectively created the middle class.

Detroit, however, is not only known for the automobile industry but also for its cultural heritage. Motown, founded by Berry Gordy, discovered and produced such musical luminaries as The Supremes, Smokey Robinson, Martha Reeves and the Vandellas, Marvin Gaye, The Jackson 5, and so many others. Additionally, Detroit is known for its legacy in gospel music including The Winans, The Clark Sisters, Commissioned, Kierra Sheard, and J. Moss.

Starting in the 1890s, Detroit became one of America's and the world's manufacturing centers. Known as Motor City—and as the arsenal of democracy during World War II—it began its post-industrial decline only in the 1970s. Manufacturing significantly strengthened the tax base, but it also did something else that would have a lingering adverse impact on public health for years to come. Without proper environmental regulation, the industrial age brought unprecedented levels of pollution. From companies dumping waste into the Great Lakes to releasing dangerous levels of toxins into the air, environmental injustice has pervaded urban centers in particular and has caused great harm. In fact, the two most polluted zip codes in Michigan are located in Detroit. These two zip codes, 48217 and 48209, are home to a Marathon Oil refinery and the Detroit Waste Water Treatment Plant.

Greenhouse gas emissions are driving climate change with significant health impacts. According to the Detroit Greenhouse Gas Inventory, conducted by the University of Michigan School of Environment and Sustainability (SEAS,

DOI: 10.4324/9780429281242-5

formerly known as School of Natural Resources and Environment), energy use for buildings and facilities (residential, commercial, institutional, industrial, and municipal) accounted for 63 percent of total citywide greenhouse gas emissions. As Detroit's Climatology Study reported, prepared by Great Lakes Integrated Sciences + Assessments (GLISA), higher greenhouse gas emissions will lead to greater incidence of heat-related illnesses (GLISA, 2017).

Detroit adults are 29 percent more likely to suffer from asthma than Michigan adults as a whole, according to a report commissioned by the Michigan Department of Health and Human Services Bureau of Disease Control, Prevention, and Epidemiology (DeGuire et al., 2016). As in many cities, Detroit is certainly experiencing the impact of climate change. Last year, there were more than 15 days with temperatures exceeding 90°F, well above the usual nine days. The airborne pollutants contribute to climate change as well as poor air quality. These are concerning weather patterns for vulnerable populations (including the elderly, young children, low-income residents, and people of color) with compromised health (such as asthma and other respiratory illnesses). These populations may not have access to affordable health care or may live in an area that is a heat island. Additionally, Detroit is experiencing more frequent and severe precipitation, which causes flooding, as stated in the Detroit Climatology Study (GLISA, 2017). This is why we must address climate change now!

Climate change now...

Detroiters Working for Environmental Justice (DWEJ) is the oldest environmental justice group in Michigan. Founded in 1994, it is an award-winning social enterprise, dedicated to making Detroit a global model of a vibrant urban center, with an emphasis on promoting sustainable redevelopment and environmental justice. From working closely with community leaders and affected residents to force the closure of a medical waste incinerator to developing the state's first green job-training program, DWEJ has been a leading voice for vulnerable communities and a trailblazer in promoting economic justice. After working for Michigan Congressman John Conyers for over a decade, I joined the staff of DWEJ in 2009.

Shortly after joining DWEJ, I had the opportunity to attend my first United Nations Framework Convention on Climate Change (COP15) in Copenhagen, Denmark, which drew close to 30,000 people from around the world. I was so honored and excited about attending this historic conference, and I was determined to make the most of this opportunity.

I believed that it was important for environmental justice leaders to meet with government officials to share our concerns and suggestions. During the COP in 2009, I contacted the White House Council of Environmental Quality, the Department of State, and the Environmental Protection Agency (EPA) to schedule a meeting. After several days, to my pleasant surprise, the meeting request was granted with the White House and EPA. During our meeting, we discussed the impact of climate change on low-income communities and communities of color. We also emphasized the importance of passing an agreement that addressed environmental justice and included aggressive climate mitigation and adaptation strategies. During one of the COP15 daily briefing sessions, I was reading a news publication that listed cities throughout the world that were committed to tackling climate change, and Detroit was not on the list. I was disturbed and began to wonder why Detroit had not made the commitment. After returning to Detroit, I began to ponder whether it made sense to forge ahead with developing a climate action plan.

The development of the city of Detroit's first climate action plan

In 2011, as the policy manager at DWEJ, I convened several stakeholders who had an interest in the environment to discuss the possibility of developing a climate action plan for the city of Detroit. They came from municipal, nonprofit, and residential backgrounds. At the time, Detroit was on the verge of bankruptcy and the appointment of an emergency manager. In 2013, the emergency manager was hired, and shortly thereafter Detroit filed for bankruptcy—the largest US municipality to do so.

During the initial stakeholder meeting, we discussed the financial state of Detroit and other pressing issues confronting the city, including serious environmental challenges which were not being adequately addressed. Two major examples of the serious environmental challenges were complaints about the city's waste incinerator and pollution in southwest Detroit. During this discussion, we asked ourselves whether it made sense to move ahead with developing the city's first climate action plan. After much debate, we agreed with a resounding "yes" to move forward. Realizing that we did not have time to wait for the local, state, or federal governments, in 2012, against many odds, we took a risk—a huge leap of faith—and launched the Detroit Climate Action Collaborative (DCAC), an initiative of DWEJ. DCAC led the development of the city of Detroit's Climate Action Plan (DCAP).

Our first task was to establish a steering committee and a research committee, which was led by Professor Larissa Larsen from Taubman College of Architecture and Urban Planning, University of Michigan. After researching various climate action plans and consulting with several cities that had already developed one—including New York (PlaNYC), Chicago, Pittsburgh, and others—we determined that we would need a cross section of perspectives and participants to develop our plan. Our desire was to ensure that varying sectors of the community would be able to implement a portion of the climate action plan and the responsibility for implementation would not rest with one person or entity. We also recognized that the implementation phase of our climate planning process would require a comprehensive fundraising plan, which is now being developed.

The Steering Committee created five work groups: Homes and Neighborhoods; Solid Waste; Public Health; Parks, Public Spaces, and Water Infrastructure; and Businesses and Institutions. We devised instructions for the work groups to establish their framework. Steps included developing mitigation and adaptation goals and short- and long-term action steps. Mitigation involved reducing emissions and stabilizing the levels of heat-trapping greenhouse gases in the atmosphere. Adaptation included adapting to the climate change already in the pipeline (NASA, n.d.).

Work groups followed the instructions of the Steering Committee and developed mitigation and adaptation goals and action steps. From 2012 to 2017, a volunteer coalition of 26 members—including businesses, community groups, universities, environmental groups, state agencies, and city leaders—was convened to address the challenges that climate change poses for Detroit. They researched and developed their frameworks, which would be the backbone of the Detroit Climate Action Plan. The Steering Committee and work group members chose the coalition members.

Through reviewing several climate action plans, we recognized 11 phases to developing a community climate action plan: (1) Structural Development, (2) Research—ongoing, (3) Fundraising—ongoing, (4) Community and Sector Engagement—partnership development, (5) Idea Exchange, (6) Framework Development, (7) Marketing—ongoing, (8) Writing, (9) Reviewing, (10) Launch, and (11) Implementation.

Most climate action plans are developed by municipalities, which makes it much easier to raise money and gain support and acceptance. Because our initiative was not led by the city but by a grassroots organization, DWEJ, we knew that we should have a strong team and to develop strong partnerships to help with capacity building, especially in the area of research. We also knew that we should attract interns/fellows to help with this evolving project, and we were grateful for their contributions. We were fortunate to be invited to apply for paid fellows through a few programs, but the majority of our interns were volunteers and participated through a college course requirement.

Research built a strong case for the urgent need to address climate change, even during a time when Detroit was experiencing so many other pressing challenges. We engaged University of Michigan scholars to conduct in-depth research and commissioned them to develop several accompanying documents to support the DCAP. We were fortunate to be included in several semester-long class projects. Our first report was the Detroit Vulnerability Assessment (Gregg at al., 2016), conducted by Professors Larissa Larsen and Eric Dueweke and their classes from Taubman College. The assessment focused on extreme weather events, including heat and flooding. Our report not only examined areas that were most susceptible to these events, but also looked at other factors, ranging from the proximity of cooling centers, to the most heat-prone areas, to income and education level of home homeowners/occupants.

The second report that was developed measured the sources of greenhouse gases at the municipal and citywide level. A greenhouse gas inventory is an essential primary step in the climate planning process. We submitted a proposal for the SEAS Master's Project to conduct a comprehensive greenhouse gas inventory and develop a report outlining the findings. This was a competitive process, but we were fortunate to be selected. The Master's Project is an inter-disciplinary capstone experience that enables SEAS master's students to develop solutions to clients' pressing real-world problems. Students work on research teams with client organizations and faculty advisors to address complex environmental issues and design innovative products. We were fortunate to work with Professors Greg Keoleian, director of the Center for Sustainable Systems, and Rosina Bierbaum from the SEAS, along with a team of five students.

After we were selected, we further defined the scope of the project and assembled the team to work with the students. This was an 18-month project that concluded with a detailed report, which was presented to Mayor Mike Duggan's office, City of Detroit department directors, and several members of DCAC. Due to a lack of space, only work group chairs were invited. Following this meeting, we formed the Mayoral Task Force on Climate Change. However, it was short-lived because of staff changes in the mayor's office.

DCAC's next report was the Detroit Climatology Study conducted by the Great Lakes Integrated Sciences + Assessments (GLISA) Center, a collaboration between the University of Michigan and Michigan State University (Detroiters Working for Environmental Justice, 2017). We partnered with GLISA to provide a historical overview of weather patterns in Detroit and future projections for extreme heat and water weather events.

Our last report, a detailed economic analysis developed by the Anderson Economic Group, examined the economic impact of 11 specific Detroit climate action plan steps by governments, businesses, and households, including planting trees, creating bike lanes, opening new parks, retrofitting buildings, and moving to renewable energy. It also highlighted the impact of investments derived from non-city government funds that resulted in new economic activity (Horwitz, 2018).

Although we recognized that research was important, we also knew that community engagement was a key component of our effort. This initiative touched people from the community. Throughout the process, we hosted four types of engagement activities: (1) focus groups conducted by the University of Michigan, which involved asking participants about the impact of climate change on their lives; (2) community conversations, held throughout the city, which invited residents to provide feedback on each of the work-group frameworks; (3) youth climate summits, in which we worked closely with Detroit public schools and other partners, to engage high school students about climate change and expose them to environmental career professionals;

and (4) business and health sector meetings, where professionals reviewed and provided input to the Businesses and Institutions and Public Health work groups' framework. Each section of the DCAP highlighted community voices, which was a snapshot of suggestions received at community gatherings.

After we received community input, the work-group framework drafts and accompanying reports were completed. It was time to start writing the DCAP. As the plan was being drafted, the writing team and I, the project coordinator, were in constant communication with the work groups and other subject-matter experts to refine our information. Drafting the plan involved a writing and design team, led by Guy Williams, president/CEO of Detroiters Working for Environmental Justice.[1]

During the writing phase, we furthered our community engagement through a series of pilot projects taken from our work group goals and short-term action steps. It was always our intent for the DCAP to be more than just another report that sat on a shelf. Instead, we wanted our plan to serve three purposes: (1) tell an important story; (2) provide an opportunity for community voices to be heard; and (3) serve as a guide and source of encouragement and empowerment. This is an ongoing process and takes the commitment of a dedicated team of volunteers.

Our first pilot project was a recommendation from the Homes and Neighborhoods work group. Through research, this group recognized that the energy burden was having a significant impact on many low-income African American families in Michigan. We also knew that energy audits not only had the ability to provide relief to many families, but could also provide a pathway out of poverty through job creation. So, we partnered with the Detroit Housing Commission to launch the Detroit Smart Neighborhood job-training course focused on energy audits. This program provided an opportunity for students to examine an existing house and collect information that was used to analyze the energy efficiency of the exterior building envelope. Public housing residents were identified to participate in the course and were trained by a few of the Home and Neighborhood work group members, which included energy efficiency experts, and an environmental certification specialist. This training was held at Lawrence Tech University Detroit Design Center in Downtown Detroit, a great location, which was recommended and secured by a work group member.

Our second pilot project was the establishment of the Detroit Climate Ambassador Program, developed by former DWEJ climate fellow Eric Douglas, who was responsible for community engagement. This undertaking was also a recommendation of the Homes and Neighborhood work group. We wanted to ensure that residents played a role in identifying and addressing climate-related challenges in their community. Our signature project was working with the Jefferson Chalmers community to address flooding. After speaking with our ambassadors and learning more about flooding challenges, we decided to launch a small green infrastructure project. To plant rain gardens and install rain barrels in an effort to reduce flooding, we partnered with community residents, the Creekside Community Development Corporation, Jefferson Chalmers Youth Connections, and University of Michigan–Dearborn assistant professor Natalie Sampson's service-learning project class. This is one of the most flood-prone areas in the city, because of a combination of aging sewer infrastructure, low topography, and the Jefferson Chalmers neighborhood's position within Detroit's combined sewer system (Kaminski et al., 2018). Since our pilot project, other initiatives have been launched to address flooding through green infrastructure.

Two of DWEJ's Climate Ambassadors, Alessandra Carreon and Drew McUsic, surveyed the homes and spoke to residents about what was required to participate. Every Saturday, over the course of several weeks, a team of volunteers helped with planting and installing rain barrels at homes. I have to admit that I do not like insects—and I don't know if I have ever seen as many of them—but I managed, and I must say this was the most rewarding project. Its purpose was to help reduce flooding risk and stormwater runoff. We were pleased with the results. Not only did this project reduce the level of flooding for some of our homeowners as well as reduce stormwater runoff, but it also lowered water bills because of the installation of green infrastructure.[2]

Our last pilot project was the development of a Sustainability Toolkit for small businesses, an action step recommendation of the Businesses and Institutions work group. Many of its members believed that small businesses, in particular, needed help to adopt sustainable business practices. Additionally, they wanted to help businesses understand the importance of becoming more sustainable. Therefore, we contacted the University of Michigan's Erb Institute to discuss the possibility of "a partnership between the Ross School of Business and the School for Environment and Sustainability, whose mission is to create a socially and environmentally sustainable world through the power of business" (Erb Institute, n.d.), to develop the Toolkit. The Toolkit helps businesses identify specific climate change risks and opportunities and then design and implement strategies to reduce their impact on the environment and adapt to inevitable changes. In particular, the Toolkit focuses on a six-step approach: (1) identify climate change risks and opportunities; (2) set ambitious but realistic goals; (3) create strategies that support your goals; (4) establish metrics that track your progress; (5) take action; and (6) improve, improve, improve.

Members of this work group understood some of the challenges that businesses encounter and were particularly concerned about the impact of sustainable practices on small businesses. For instance, the energy burden can present a real danger to the operational success of a small business. In fact, the National Small Business Association Energy Survey reported that more than 50 percent of businesses surveyed said future energy costs were a major business concern (NSBA, 2011). The survey also indicated that a lack of capital was the primary reason for not making businesses more energy efficient. The DCAC

Businesses and Institutions work group convened the first Small Business Summit, and a second was convened by a team of Detroit business leaders.

Our last project before the launch of the Detroit Climate Action Plan was the film *From the Bottom Up: Climate Action in Detroit*, an important addition to our climate action planning development process. After viewing several films about climate change, I did not see any that focused on its impact on urban communities, so I convened a meeting with award-winning Detroit-based film director Diane Checklich, University of Michigan–Dearborn assistant professor Natalie Sampson, and research assistant Jessica Doan to develop the film.

Serving as the coproducers, Sampson and I launched the film at a green carpet event at the Charles H. Wright Museum of African American History on October 24, 2017. Following the screening, we held a panel discussion with some of our Detroit Climate Ambassador members and leaders who represented the business, residential, academic, and nonprofit sectors. The purpose of the panel was to discuss the impact of climate change on various business sectors and the importance of everyone playing a role.

The purpose of the film was to highlight the unique climate challenges experienced by those who reside in low-income communities and communities of color. The widely publicized film has been shown in community meetings as well as at the American Public Health Association annual meeting and has attracted a diverse audience.[3] We are pleased with the response we have received from this film, along with the momentum it is building around addressing climate change, and will continue to show it at different community events.

From the Bottom Up: Climate Action in Detroit documents the challenges and opportunities for developing a cross-sector plan to mitigate and adapt to greenhouse gas emissions in ways that protect residents' health across Detroit's changing landscapes. At the end of the screening, we were proud to announce that the Detroit Climate Action Plan would be launched the following day at a press conference. It was a full house. Many people were invited to attend the press conference, including the DCAC Steering Committee, work group members, residents, and government and business leaders. We were very pleased with the attendance at the press conference and many of our partners and friends were there to support the launch of this historic effort.

The DCAP outlines specific goals and action steps that will better prepare Detroit to endure the challenges of climate change. In particular, it calls for a reduction in greenhouse gas emissions, as well as improving the energy efficiency and durability of homes. The plan also outlines key strategies for a well-managed zero waste stream that promotes universal recycling and mitigates greenhouse gases and calls for updating citywide and agency response plans to ensure they address the public health risks of climate change. Lastly, it focuses on strategies that use parks as carbon sinks and open spaces to control stormwater runoff. At the time of writing, we do not know how long it will take to complete the long-term action steps.

After many drafts, we launched the first Detroit Climate Action Plan on October 26, 2017, during a press conference at the Oakland Avenue Urban Farm. Following the announcement, we held a reception in the farm's greenhouse to celebrate our success. Even as we were celebrating, we knew our work was not finished.

Earlier during the planning process, I formed a policy team to develop a city climate ordinance. Attorney Nicholas Leonard, executive director of the Great Lakes Environmental Law Center, and his team of students drafted the ordinance to set greenhouse gas reduction targets and regularly require a greenhouse gas inventory, among other important things. In July 2019, the City Council passed the Greenhouse Gas Ordinance, which established greenhouse gas reduction targets for municipal operations as well as a citywide goal. As well as the inventory, the ordinance requires an annual report to the City Council outlining how reduction targets are being met.

Lessons learned: our challenges

As a person of Christian faith, I knew that part of my mission in life was to lead the development of Detroit's Climate Action Plan. We experienced many challenges while developing this historic document, including lack of financial support for capacity building, an uncertain future for the city of Detroit, and lack of a local precedent to follow. Capturing community input was also difficult. We played around with several words before settling on "Community Conversations". We wanted our conversations to be interactive. To accommodate participants, we modified our meetings as needed, holding them in different communities throughout the city. Some were held during the day, others in the evening. We also provided food, because we knew that people were coming from work. This strategy worked well.

We hired a community resource agency to help us develop a community engagement plan. The agency provided a list of other community agencies to help us recruit people to participate in our Community Conversations. The agency also provided training for our Climate Ambassadors at a local café. The purpose of the training was to prepare the ambassadors to talk to their neighbors about climate change and how it was affecting their community. Following the training, we held two community workshops: Recycling and Green Infrastructure. Residents were taught the importance of recycling, given a free recycling bin, and learned about the significance of green infrastructure, and how to build a rain garden and install a rain barrel.

Although developing a comprehensive climate action plan was rewarding, it was also exhausting, not for the faint of heart. Prepare for pushback from various entities because they may not support the involvement of a particular partner or suggestions from other team members, and some will leave the effort to either pursue other opportunities, because they no longer have the time to commit, or because they have lost interest. However, being reminded of my vision for leading the development of a climate action plan compelled me to stay the course.

Implementation

The climate planning process has several phases, of which one of the most important is implementation. Since the launch of the DCAC in 2012, the city has had a Sustainability Office. Although I am no longer with DWEJ, as chair of the Detroit Green Task Force Climate Action Committee and president/CEO of Future Insight Consulting, LLC (FIC), I am leading the implementation of three areas of the Detroit Climate Action Plan: Businesses and Institutions, Public Health, and Homes and Neighborhoods. After reviewing many of the environmentally related projects in Detroit, it was determined that these three areas were not being fully addressed as detailed in our climate action plan. Many who are working on the implementation phase also worked on developing the plan. Currently, we are in the process of prioritizing the plan's near-term action steps for these three areas. We will then select the top five near-term steps and develop an implementation plan.

In my work on climate change as president/CEO of Future Insight Consulting, LLC, which focuses on corporate sustainability, advocacy, and coalition building, I was recently invited to chair the Detroit Climate Action Sub-Committee. Led by Council Member Scott Benson, it is part of the Detroit City Council Green Task Force. In this role, I am working with stakeholders to plan the implementation of the Detroit Climate Action Plan, pass the Detroit Climate Ordinance, and develop an education and outreach program to further engage Detroiters in addressing climate change.

Teamwork makes the dream work

This work would not have been possible without the contribution of many people, especially our project coordinator, who led the Detroit Youth Climate Summits, conducted research, and helped with overall management of the project; Eric Douglas, climate fellow, who developed and launched the Detroit Climate Ambassador Program and organized community outreach; Khalil Ligon, climate leadership fellow; the New Organizing Institute (Now Wellstone Action), which laid the groundwork for the Detroit Climate Ambassador Program, and did community outreach and helped with research; Courtney Chennault, who helped with research for the climate ordinance and did community outreach; Guy Williams, president/CEO of DWEJ, who allowed me to work on this project for six years and assemble a team to gather all of the information that had been developed in order to write the Detroit Climate Action Plan.[4]

I am grateful for all of the working group members and other supporters who stayed with us through every delay, valley, and mountain-top experience. To God be the Glory!

Notes

1   For a complete list of those involved in this lengthy process, visit the DWEJ website at https://detroitenvironmentaljustice.org/climate-action-plan/.
2   This is not an ongoing project because of lack of funding.
3   To view the film, contact DWEJ at https://detroitenvironmentaljustice.org/.
4   For a complete list of those who participated in the process of developing the DCAP, visit https://detroitenvironmentaljustice.org/.

References

DeGuire, Peter, Binxin Cao, Lauren Wisnieski, Doug Strane, Robert Wahl, Sarah Lyon-Callo, and Erika Garcia. *Excerpts from Detroit: The Current Status of the Asthma Burden.* Michigan Department of Health and Human Services Bureau of Disease Control, Prevention, and Epidemiology, March 2016, www.michigan.gov/asthma.

Erb Institute. "About the Institute," n.d., accessed July 3, 2019, https://erb.umich.edu/about/.

GLISA (Great Lakes Integrated Sciences + Assessments), *The Potential Impacts of Climate Change on Detroit, Michigan,* 2017, https://glisa.umich.edu/media/files/projects/DCAC/DCAC_Climate_Impacts.pdf.

Gregg, Kelly, Peter McGrath, Sarah Nowaczyk, Andrew Perry, Karen Spangler, Taylor Traub, and Ben VanGessel. *Foundations for Community Climate Action: Defining Climate Change Vulnerability in Detroit.* University of Michigan Taubman College of Architecture & Urban Planning, December 2012.

Horwitz, Jason. *Economic Impacts of the Detroit Climate Action Plan.* Anderson Economic Group, July 2018, https://detroitenvironmentaljustice.org/wp-content/uploads/2018/07/DCAPImpact_Report_FINALv5-2.pdf.

Kaminski, Michael, Ruiyang Li, Robert Haarer, Zhen Yi, Pojing Liu, and Jing Bu. *Stormwater Management in Southeast Detroit: Adaptive and Contextually Informed Green Infrastructure Strategies.* Master's Project, University of Michigan, April 2018, https://deepblue.lib.umich.edu/handle/2027.42/106566.

NASA. "Global Climate Change, Vital Signs of the Planet, Solutions Mitigation and Adaptation, Responding to Climate Change," n.d., https://climate.nasa.gov/solutions/adaptation-mitigation/.

NSBA. *2011 Energy Survey,* 2011, https://www.nsba.biz/docs/2011_energy_survey.pdf.

Chapter 5

Business

Building climate-resilient supply chains (IBM supply chain)

Diana Dierks and Louis Ferretti

Collaboration for climate action in the IBM supply chain

In today's business landscape, a company's corporate responsibility strategy is becoming as visible—and potentially as important—as the company's financial and business strategies. In addition, our interconnected world means no company is an island. There is growing expectation that companies go beyond their own operations to setting standards for their suppliers as well, to drive sustainability in their own supply chains. Moreover, a company's brand image can be negatively affected if any one of its suppliers has poor ethical, social, or environmental performance. As a result, a company's supply chain has an increasing impact on and represents a potential risk to a company's reputation and leadership. To succeed in addressing such expectations and harness the opportunity to affect positive change, a company and its suppliers need to put programs in place and work in a collaborative fashion to achieve social and environmental objectives.

In 1969, Thomas J. Watson, Jr., then CEO of IBM, included the following commitment among IBM's "Basic Beliefs & Principles":

> We accept our responsibilities as a corporate citizen in community, national, and world affairs; we serve our interests best when we serve the public interest. ... We want to be at the forefront of those companies which are working to make our world a better place.
>
> (IBM, n.d.c.)

These principles led IBM to embark on a comprehensive approach to corporate responsibility that aligns with IBM's enduring values and maximizes the positive change that it can effect around the world. Its approach has led to advances in social and environmental responsibility over the decades. For instance, IBM's long-standing commitment to environmental responsibility traces its roots back to 1971, when it published its first formal corporate environmental policy (IBM, n.d.a), followed by its first corporate energy policy in

DOI: 10.4324/9780429281242-6

1974. Programs supporting these policies have been embedded within IBM's corporate-wide environmental programs and global environmental management system since that time. Figure 5.1 provides a small sampling of IBM's environmental leadership milestones throughout its history, several of which we will expand upon later in the chapter.

As IBM advanced its environmental and social performance, it saw the need to encourage suppliers to pursue a similar course. From a procurement perspective, more than managing spend, IBM knew it had a responsibility to hold itself and its suppliers to high standards of behavior. This goes beyond complying with applicable laws and regulations and entails a strong commitment to working with suppliers to encourage sound practices and develop sound global markets. To this end, IBM worked collaboratively within its own organization and externally across industry and consortia to establish a number of programs to address the social and environmental aspects of its supply chain comprehensively, including climate protection. Here, we will discuss two of these programs: (1) IBM's Supply Chain Social Responsibility, and (2) IBM's Social and Environmental Management System supplier requirements.

There are many interdependencies in IBM's organization, with an important collaboration between IBM Supply Chain Global Procurement (Procurement), Corporate Environmental Affairs (CEA), and Corporate Social Responsibility. For instance, IBM CEA directs environmental affairs programs for the company, including strategy and direction in pursuit of environmental leadership and sustainability, across all aspects of IBM's global business operations. The business operations groups, such as Procurement, take CEA's direction and determine the optimal execution of its environmental management system. Feedback loops are built in for continual improvement on both fronts, harnessing a collaborative relationship between CEA and Procurement operations. This collaboration has led to a tight alignment between the two organizations' leadership to execute IBM's environmental responsibilities in the supply chain. The evolution of the two programs—Supply Chain Social Responsibility and the Social and Environmental Management System—did not happen in a linear manner; rather, they evolved and progressed along with the conditions, risks, and opportunities of the business.

In 1997, IBM became the first major multinational company to earn a single global registration to the International Organization for Standardization's (ISO) 14001 environmental management systems (EMS) standard: a voluntary international standard that identifies the elements of an EMS needed for an organization to manage its impact on the environment effectively. Its objective is to integrate the EMS with overall business management processes, so that environmental considerations are incorporated into business decisions. IBM earned this credential within just one year of the finalized first edition of the standard, in part due to the results already delivered under the company's environmental policy and the early implementation of IBM's environmental management programs.

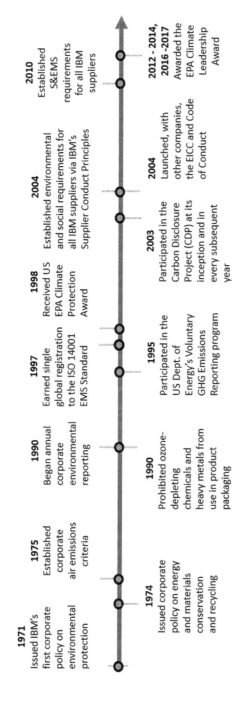

Figure 5.1 Highlights of IBM's environmental leadership history
Source: the author/IBM.

Seeing IBM's supply chain as an extension of its own business operations, the company issued a letter to its suppliers in 1998, encouraging them to also adopt the ISO 14001 standard. It was a recommendation, not a requirement, and few supplier advances were made. It was, however, an early attempt in the right direction.

The IBM Supply Chain Social Responsibility Program

In the early 2000s, IBM executives such as John Paterson, IBM's chief procurement officer at the time, and others saw that a large corporation like IBM needed a well-defined code of conduct across its suppliers. This was stimulated in part by changes in IBM's business. The company had divested significant manufacturing operations (electronic card assembly and test) to third-party electronic manufacturing service providers. This caused IBM's procurement spending to increase as the company was now buying from third parties rather than manufacturing these products in-house. Much of this sourcing expansion was in the Asia-Pacific region, where awareness of supply chain social responsibility was in its early stages of development. IBM wanted to ensure suppliers operated responsibly with respect to working conditions, health, safety, environment, wages and benefits, etc., and it was ready to lead such change. In a 2004 letter to IBM suppliers, Paterson stated, "Our company's purchase base is a unique resource and comes with a responsibility to hold ourselves—and our suppliers—to high standards of behavior." With that communication, IBM established requirements for all its suppliers via the IBM Supplier Conduct Principles and supporting audit program. The Supplier Conduct Principles covered the following 13 elements:

1) Forced or involuntary labor
2) Child labor
3) Wages and benefits
4) Working hours
5) Nondiscrimination
6) Respect and dignity
7) Freedom of association
8) Health and safety
9) Protection of the environment
10) Laws, including regulations and other legal requirements
11) Ethical dealings
12) Communications
13) Monitoring/record-keeping (IBM, 2004)

This formalized IBM's commitment to corporate responsibility requirements for suppliers. Suppliers were required to sign a binding agreement that they would comply with the Supplier Conduct Principles. However, it was the auditing of suppliers and education efforts that demonstrated an even greater commitment by IBM. Essential to the corporation's goal of making supply chain responsibility part of the normal course of business was educating its supplier-facing employees to help suppliers improve their performance.

With suppliers in more than 80 countries at that time, IBM focused its initial audits on locations where it had a concentration of suppliers in emerging markets and then expanded the geographic scope in subsequent years. IBM engaged the help of a firm that specialized in corporate responsibility audits, using trained local professionals to conduct audits at the suppliers' factories, offices, and distribution hubs. Using a combination of face-to-face interviews with plant managers and employees, and a review of records and policies, the audits were designed to reveal a comprehensive picture of how a facility operates and to help uncover any problems that existed.

Any noncompliance required a supplier-generated root cause and corrective action plan to be submitted, for IBM review, and a re-audit to be scheduled. Having the supplier generate its own corrective action plan encouraged it to take ownership of its own progress and devise realistic solutions that work for its business. For significant noncompliance findings, such as worker safety, IBM demanded immediate action and correction. In general, rather than ending the business relationship with noncompliant suppliers—which tended to limit the incentive for a company to improve and may have led to facility closures—IBM's goal was to build success in supplier responsibility. Further, as validated by re-audit findings, IBM found that meaningful changes in one supplier can spread to others and that the corrective action plans paved the way for improved business practices that could lead to sustainable improvements.

The Supplier Conduct Principles distinguished IBM as a leading company adopting a holistic approach to supply chain responsibility, seeing suppliers as an extension of the business. IBM gained traction and alignment with its enforcement of the principles and supporting audit program. Many suppliers successfully implemented policies and practices in support of these principles, improving their performance in the areas of social and environmental responsibility. For example, during re-audits of IBM's suppliers in Mexico in 2006, first audited in 2004–5, the findings showed a 95 percent improvement in compliance.

For suppliers who failed to demonstrate compliance, IBM worked with the supplier to improve its degree of compliance, at times involving an extended implementation plan period. For those that continued to be unable, IBM discontinued the business relationship as a result.

The majority of the Supplier Conduct Principles concentrated on social requirements, though they also contained environmental requirements. Specifically, the Protection of the Environment principle stated that IBM suppliers will operate in a manner that is protective of the environment. At a minimum, it required supplier compliance with all applicable environmental laws, regulations, and standards, such as chemical and waste management, recycling, air emissions controls, environmental permits, and environmental reporting. Beyond that, it stated that suppliers "should *strive* to implement management systems to meet these requirements" (IBM, 2004). This continued along the path started in the 1998 letter to suppliers encouraging adoption of ISO 14001; with the word "strive," however, it still signaled that implementation of a management system was desired but not required.

During its first round of supplier audits using the Supplier Conduct Principles, IBM was contacted by several companies within the electronics sector to begin a joint discussion on supply chain corporate responsibility. The rationale was simple: IBM, HP, Dell, and several of their contract manufacturing suppliers, including Celestica, Flextronics, Jabil, Sanmina, and Solectron, understood that supply chain responsibility would have a greater impact if our companies collaborated. The direction IBM had set with the Supplier Conduct Principles was significant, yet the company realized such leadership in an interconnected global marketplace should include finding a way to positively influence all supply chains, not just its own. Indeed, each of these companies had been working individually to create and execute guiding principles that reflect each organization's values.

The discussion formalized, and in 2004 a total of 12 companies (Celestica, Cisco, Dell, Flex, HP, IBM, Intel, Jabil, Microsoft, Sanmina, Solectron, and Sony) founded the Electronic Industry Citizenship Coalition (EICC) to create a unified approach and a common set of standards for responsible behavior across the industry. The original group of major electronics brands and first-tier suppliers created what was known as the EICC Code of Conduct, which was similar to IBM's Supplier Conduct Principles, and was the first collaboration on corporate responsibility among the electronics industry on a global scale. The EICC Code of Conduct paved the way for a standards-based approach for monitoring suppliers' performance across several areas of social responsibility, including labor practices, health and safety, environmental, ethics, and management systems. Central to the collaboration of the EICC is the reality of interwoven supply chains.

The founding member companies committed to applying the EICC Code of Conduct in their own operations and with their suppliers. As IBM already had its own incumbent audit system, it took a period of time for IBM to make the complete transition in its supplier audit protocols. IBM started the transition to the EICC Code of Conduct and associated audit process for its own direct procurement supply base in 2010, while continuing to use the IBM Supplier Conduct Principles for its indirect procurement suppliers. By March 2013, IBM fully adopted the EICC Code of Conduct as IBM's own supplier code of conduct, superseding the Supplier Conduct Principles, which had been used from 2004 to 2013. This milestone was achieved through strong collaboration between the EICC and IBM, led by John Gabriel, manager of IBM's supply chain social responsibility program.

By IBM adopting the EICC Code of Conduct as its own, the minimum social responsibility standards it expects from suppliers as a condition of doing business match those of other member companies. This gives more consistency and traction to the requirements. The benefits translate to the supplier as well. Foremost, suppliers benefit by having a single common code of standards across the industry. Often, a factory producing for IBM will also be producing for several other companies. If those companies are using the same code of conduct, the expectations for that factory will be clear. In addition, it can reduce the number of audits and therefore supplier fatigue. An EICC audit score is good for two years, and the audit findings can be shared by the supplier with its other customers who approach the company for an EICC audit within that time, in lieu of additional audits. Thus, the combined influence of a coalition of companies can drive efficiencies in addition to changes in supplier performance.

Although the EICC Code of Conduct originated with the electronics industry in mind, it is applicable to and used by many other industries, as electronics are now a key component in many sectors such as automotive, retail, and toy companies. Further, the EICC Code of Conduct may be voluntarily adopted by any business in the electronics sector and subsequently applied by that business to its supply chain and subcontractors, including providers of contract labor. In October 2017, the EICC leadership reflected its expanded reach and impact across a wider range of industries and companies by rebranding itself the Responsible Business Alliance (RBA). The RBA Code of Conduct, now in its sixth version, defines 43 requirements across the following five dimensions:

1) Labor
2) Health and safety
3) Environmental
4) Ethics
5) Management systems (Responsible Business Alliance, n.d.)

The code's environmental requirements have evolved over the years, with energy consumption and greenhouse gas emissions tracking added to RBA's Code of Conduct in 2014 as climate change became more prominent for member companies. IBM, via its Social and Environmental Management System (S&EMS) requirements, discussed later in this chapter, had already required its suppliers to have an environmental management system in place since 2010, including the measurement, reduction goals, and performance disclosure of greenhouse gas emissions.

The RBA Code of Conduct states that companies adopting the code "must regard it as a total supply chain initiative" (ibid.). It requires a process to communicate code requirements to suppliers and to monitor supplier compliance. IBM requires its suppliers to sign a letter of agreement that they will comply with the provisions contained in the RBA Code of Conduct. The company actively monitors suppliers' performance via supplier audits (through certified third parties) to determine whether they are complying. IBM's supplier-assessment activity follows the methodology developed by the RBA, under which audited suppliers create and submit a Corrective Action Plan (CAP) for all nonconformances discovered in an audit. This requirement is a core tenet of IBM's supplier management system and is fully supported by IBM Procurement and its executive team. The CAP enables the audited company to create meaningful targeted improvements and later to test effectiveness through a re-audit.

Continuous focus on social responsibility and supplier commitment has driven meaningful improvements over the years. Assessing suppliers against the RBA Code of Conduct provides them with objective, third-party evidence to determine whether their operations are compliant or need improvement, and how. In the case of working hours, comparing results over the near- and mid-term, we can see improved results. IBM's 2018 Corporate Responsibility Report (IBM, 2019) shows the combined major and minor nonconformance findings for working hours declined to 13 percent in 2018, down from 16 percent in 2017 and 20 percent in 2016.

Audits are a valuable tool, and when combined with long-term supplier relationships and agreements to invest in improvements toward code compliance, they can help drive relative long-term improvement. For instance, the initial on-site RBA audit of a packaging solutions supplier's facility conducted in 2016 received a low score (83/200). The findings were predominantly health and safety-related (for example, worker exposure to potential safety hazards) with a few from environmental, labor, and management systems (such as no process to ensure that environmentally related licenses are periodically reviewed and are up to date; no process to ensure that next-tier suppliers implement the Code of Conduct). With a score of less than 200, the supplier was required to complete a CAP upon release of the final audit report and submit the CAP to IBM for review, discussion, and approval. Once the CAP actions were completed, the re-audit was scheduled, and the supplier scored 194/200. The supplier then scored a perfect 200/200 in its subsequent 2018 audit.

As reported in IBM's 2018 Corporate Responsibility Report (IBM, 2019), 46 percent of re-audited suppliers addressed all code compliance issues after completing their re-audit cycle. This significant achievement shows both the value of going through the full RBA process as well as suppliers' commitment to investing in lasting improvements. IBM provides guidance to suppliers throughout the process, including IBM-authored educational materials as well as directing suppliers to selected curricula in the RBA Learning Academy and tracking their completion. IBM Procurement works with suppliers who have outstanding issues following their re-audits, and reviews audit results with IBM Procurement's executive team monthly.

Over the last dozen or so years, almost 2,000 on-site supplier audits have been conducted on behalf of IBM. The company's goal is to work with its suppliers to foster full compliance as those suppliers, in turn, apply the standards to downstream suppliers engaged in the production of goods and services for IBM suppliers, thereby elevating the performance of the whole supply chain.

IBM's Supply Chain Social and Environmental Management System

In 2009, after the previous early initiatives encouraging suppliers to have environmental management systems in place, IBM was ready to strengthen its position with formal requirements for adhering to them. Amid the progress being made in supply chain responsibility with the Supplier Conduct Principles and RBA (then EICC) Code of Conduct, IBM saw a need to advance its supply chain environmental programs to the next level. It recognized the growing imperative for environmental and corporate responsibility across supply chains, underscoring that effective environmental management makes good business sense. The requirements in place at that point had been strong on supply chain social responsibility but with a lighter focus on environmental issues, so the leadership in IBM CEA and Procurement realized they needed something additional to address the level of environmental responsibility that IBM expects from its suppliers. The goal was to have requirements that could apply to all IBM suppliers and would drive them to actively manage their environmental responsibility and performance and help build their capability.

The mission was driven at the senior executive level, jointly by the vice president of CEA and product safety, Wayne Balta, and the then-chief procurement officer, John Paterson. Together they asked their teams to determine how to extend the tenets of IBM's environmental management system to IBM's supply base. In 2009, the director of IBM CEA, Edan Dionne, and Louis Ferretti, leader of supply chain risk, environmental compliance, and social responsibility, authored a plan for launching such a program. The team went through several iterations as it refined the scope, based on feedback from a committee of IBM executives. All involved wanted to ensure a robust, auditable, and specific—yet all-inclusive—set of requirements. One of the decision points was whether the requirements should be for an EMS only, or should also include social responsibility elements. The team determined that the optimal strategy would be for the new requirements to cover the two areas—environmental and social—as both are integral elements of the responsible management system IBM expected of suppliers. The idea was to form a comprehensive, single-umbrella approach that connected IBM's existing strong social responsibility program with the new equally strong environmental program. The team presented its plan to senior vice presidents in IBM Procurement, and having gained their support, it was ready to launch.

In February 2010, IBM's chief procurement officer announced in a letter to its 28,000 suppliers in more than 90 countries that they would be required to deploy and sustain a corporate responsibility and environmental management system; measure environmental performance (at minimum energy consumption, greenhouse gas emissions, and waste management) and establish voluntary environmental goals to improve performance; publicly disclose results associated with these goals and other environmental aspects of the management system; and communicate these requirements to any suppliers material to IBM's products, parts, or services. A public announcement was made in April 2010 via joint communications from Paterson and Balta. It immediately received positive press from the likes of the *Harvard Business Review* and *The New York Times*, highlighting the significant step IBM made in "greening" the supply chain. In an interview with *The New York Times*, Balta said, "Our overall interest is to systemize environmental management and sustainability across our global supply chain so it helps our suppliers build their own capacity in a way that's not only good for the environment but their business" (Woody, 2010).

And so, IBM's S&EMS supplier requirements program was established, necessitating that all IBM suppliers execute the following requirements:

1) Establish a corporate social responsibility and environmental management system that is defined, deployed, and sustainable and that identifies significant aspects of the supplier's intersections with these matters, including those articulated in the Responsible Business Alliance (RBA) Code of Conduct.[1] The supplier must be able to demonstrate that such a management system is in place and is deployed at their sites where work for IBM is performed, such that should IBM choose to conduct an audit, either by IBM or an IBM-directed third party, of a supplier's corporate social responsibility program and/or supplier's environmental program, the supplier will be able to demonstrate complete compliance to all elements of the RBA Code of Conduct;

2) Establish programs (within the supplier's management system) to control operations that intersect with the above matters and that confirm their compliance with applicable law, regulation, and any particular contractual requirements related to IBM;

3) Monitor/measure supplier's environmental performance and have established voluntary environmental goals to track and improve upon environmental performance, and, where applicable include at a minimum each of the following environmental aspects:
   a) energy conservation
   b) waste management and recycling
   c) scope 1 and scope 2 greenhouse gas (GHG) emissions*

4) Set voluntary environmental goals to achieve positive results associated with the supplier's significant environmental aspects, where applicable, and include at a minimum one goal in each of the three aspects cited in requirement 3 above;

1   When the S&EMS supplier requirements were announced in 2010, the Responsible Business Alliance (RBA) was called Electronics Industry Citizenship Coalition (EICC).

5) Publicly disclose results associated with the above-mentioned voluntary environmental goals and other environmental aspects from the management system, including any regulatory fines or penalties that may have occurred;

6) Train employees who are responsible for the performing/monitoring/measuring/reporting of environmental performance, assuring the appropriate skill-level and competency;

7) As part of the supplier's management system, conduct self-assessments and audits as well as management reviews of the supplier's system;

Cascade the above set of (seven) IBM requirements to the supplier's own suppliers that perform work that is material to the products, parts, and/or services supplied to IBM.

★ Scope 1 greenhouse gas emissions: direct emissions generated by the company. Scope 2 greenhouse gas emissions: indirect emissions that are associated with the generation of electricity that is purchased and consumed by the company.[2]

(IBM, n.d.b)

These requirements are unique within the industry, due to their systemic approach and emphasis on the integration of responsible management systems into the core of each supplier's business. The requirements do not prescribe; they address *what* suppliers should do, but not *how*. The requirements deliberately avoid prescribing a particular type of management system or public reporting tool to allow suppliers the flexibility to develop the systems that work best in their particular industries and contexts. This flexibility is key for the requirements to apply to all IBM suppliers. Taking public disclosure as an example, there are many ways a company might publicly report its performance: publish an annual corporate report on its environmental performance; simply display the performance on its website and perhaps update it more frequently; report its emissions annually via the Carbon Disclosure Project; follow the Global Reporting Initiative reporting framework or report via OneReport; and so on. IBM does not mandate the method used, as long as the company meets the S&EMS requirements.

The 2010 announcement also marked the establishment of IBM's own integrated S&EMS within IBM Supply Chain Global Procurement, which combines into a single management system its environmental and social supply

---

2   Scope1 greenhouse gas emissions are Direct GHG emissions. Direct GHG emissions occur from sources that are owned or controlled by the company, for example, emissions from combustion in owned or controlled boilers, furnaces, vehicles, etc. and emissions from chemical production in owned or controlled process equipment. Scope 2 greenhouse gas emissions are indirect GHG emissions attributable to electricity production. Scope 2 accounts for GHG emissions from the generation of purchased electricity consumed by the company. Purchased electricity is defined as electricity that is purchased or otherwise brought into the organizational boundaries of the company.

chain compliance programs. Both are integral elements of the management system to which IBM expects suppliers to adhere. Therefore, by establishing a single-umbrella management system for the two requirements programs (the existing Supplier Conduct Principles/RBA Code of Conduct and the new S&EMS supplier requirements), it combines each of their strengths and together forms a comprehensive approach to the full scope of social and environmental standards for IBM's supply chain.

In late 2011, the IBM team worked to socialize and amplify the S&EMS program outside of the organization. IBM arranged a Supply Chain Sustainability Summit in Washington, DC, and invited a representative group of IBM suppliers and thought leaders in supply chain management from industry, academia, and the not-for-profit sector to share their experiences. The objective of the summit was to bring together a number of companies—a mix of large and small suppliers across various industries and countries that had implemented comprehensive management systems—to participate in roundtable discussions and learn from each other's challenges and insights. Participants shared information about current and potential benefits from taking a systematic approach toward their management systems. The group shared experiences and resources to increase awareness of the growing importance of corporate social and environmental programs. Overall, the summit exhibited and validated a willingness, across industries, to put programs in place and confirmed that social and environmental responsibility had a permanent place in corporate cultures.

IBM's S&EMS supplier requirements program has received a steady stream of recognition and awards from industry groups, peers, academia, and the press. The Institute of Supply Management honored IBM in 2011 with the first-ever Award for Excellence in Supply Management, in the Sustainability category (SDC Executive, 2011). Later, IBM received the 2013 EPA Climate Leadership Award, citing both the company's ambitious emissions reduction goals and its leadership in setting requirements for suppliers to measure, disclose, and reduce their operational greenhouse gas emissions (EPA Center for Corporate Climate Leadership, 2013). And IBM won the 2017 Circle of Excellence Award from the Distribution Business Management Association for its profound commitment to environmental and social responsibility, highlighting the S&EMS supplier requirements program (Distribution Business Management Association, n.d.).

Challenges and benefits

Implementing and maintaining Supply Chain Social Responsibility and S&EMS supplier requirement programs has not come without challenges. There can be a lack of awareness and understanding by suppliers, especially in growth market countries. Regardless of geography, organizations often encounter suppliers who categorically think such requirements do not apply to them. Further, the scale of a global enterprise with a large number of employees (hundreds of buyers across approximately 80 countries), and thousands of suppliers, poses a challenge in program execution.

With strong support at the executive management through regional levels of procurement, IBM has sought to drive performance and compliance with these programs. Policies and corporate instructions set at the CEA level, bolstered by procurement policies and practices, set the guidelines for ongoing execution. In addition to policy, leadership ensures that budget, staffing, and education resources are provided. All of this is incorporated into the management system, employing the plan-do-check-act model and certified to the ISO 14001:2015 standard. Since the launch of these programs, a strong focus on education has been in place, educating both IBM procurement staff and their suppliers. All employees in IBM's global procurement organization complete training courses on both the S&EMS and Supply Chain Social Responsibility (RBA Code of Conduct) programs. Moreover, IBM regularly provides materials and conducts education and targeted training to update employees on related policies, processes, and practices. In approaching it as a partnership to help suppliers on their journey, communication and setting expectations are key. The IBM procurement staff who have relationships with suppliers are best suited to provide tailored education to the supplier, as needed, to help achieve compliance.

IBM's programs are not box-checking exercises nor just "nice to haves." Rather, they are requirements that can benefit the supplier. Having an effective environment management program helps a supplier understand its resource dependencies and consumption. It can help them identify operational efficiencies and areas for improvement. Moreover, transparency of programs not only drives performance but also allows companies to showcase their efforts. In a recent example, the IBM S&EMS team engaged with a new mobile computing services supplier who, during initial assessment, was uncertain about setting environmental goals and how to publicly disclose environmental performance as required by IBM. The company guided the supplier on areas for improvement and conducted several checkpoints, where the supplier presented its initiatives that were already underway but not publicized. These included LED light bulb conversion and other facility energy efficiency projects at certain locations, and a device buy-back program to reduce landfill waste at product end of life, and more. The supplier formed and executed a plan for full compliance. The result was an improved Corporate Social Responsibility page on its website that not only demonstrates transparency and continual improvement in the company's social and environmental performance, but further allows the supplier to showcase its initiatives and achievements, covering its products, services and facilities, for a wide audience including clients and investors.

Based on IBM's own experience over many decades, sound environmental management leads to direct improvements to the bottom line, be it savings from increased resource efficiency (such as conserving energy, water, and materials), lowering costs by minimizing waste, or addressing regulatory requirements to avoid penalties. Further, conducting business in an ethical manner and making a positive social impact protects and improves a company's reputation. Effective management systems in these areas can mitigate business risks and better prepare the business for the future.

As suppliers integrate twenty-first-century corporate responsibility and environmental management systems into their businesses, they are more attractive to others. The customer inquiries and requests for proposals IBM receives almost always include questions about the company's social and environmental programs and, increasingly, that of the supply chain. It benefits IBM to highlight its robust Supply Chain Social Responsibility and S&EMS Supplier Requirements programs. The same goes for addressing corporate sustainability surveys and even board of director meetings where supply chain risk is a topic. Customers, investors, and shareholders want sustainable supply chains, as do employees and recruits who are passionate about working for a sustainable company.

Climate protection

IBM does not require its suppliers to do anything it does not demand of itself. It has sustained a corporate responsibility and environmental management system for decades, controlling its operations and compliance obligations, managing its continued evolution, setting and advancing goals, measuring and reporting performance, training staff, conducting self-assessments and audits, and requiring such responsibility of its suppliers. In the area of climate protection, for instance, IBM has set and achieved multiple generations of climate protection goals over several decades, including energy conservation and the procurement of renewable energy. From 1990 through 2018, IBM conserved 7.5 million MWh of electricity, avoiding 4.5 million metric tons of CO_2 emissions and saving $632 million.

IBM believes results in greenhouse gas (GHG) emissions reduction are directly achieved when each enterprise takes responsibility to address its own emissions and improve its energy efficiency. As such, part of IBM's strategy to reduce GHG emissions includes requiring IBM suppliers to track energy use and GHG emissions, set reduction plans, and publicly report results, all as part of their environmental management system. This is driven via IBM's requirement that all IBM first-tier suppliers develop a management system compliant with IBM's S&EMS requirements and RBA Code of Conduct, for example to monitor Scope 1 and Scope 2 GHG emissions, set goals, and report performance. The reach is furthered by the requirement that suppliers cascade IBM's S&EMS requirements to their next-tier suppliers who perform work that is material to the goods or services being supplied to IBM. As companies gain an understanding of their energy use and GHG emissions, and commit to improvement goals and disclosure, they are likely to act to improve their performance in these areas.

Conclusion

It is critical that organizations understand their responsibility in relation to climate, environment, and sustainability and manage it both within their own operations and with their extended supply chain. IBM recognizes that its sizeable purchasing power is a unique resource and has taken the opportunity to influence responsible supply chain performance. Such an understanding of its responsibility has led IBM to establish environmental and social requirements for all its suppliers, contribute to the formation and evolution of industry standards and codes of conduct, and lead by example, with programs and applications of technology that increase supply chain responsibility. Rather than wait for industry standards or legislation to evolve, IBM has chosen to act now and influence an ecologically conscious, responsible, and sustainable supply chain.

For other companies looking to act, the experience at IBM suggests the following guidelines to aid success:

- Secure the support of a well-positioned executive (or executives) who has the vision and the authority to initiate a program and oversee its execution
- Ensure funding to build tools and develop a staff of subject-matter experts
- Be prepared not just to establish a program but to sustain it; maintaining a program can be more challenging than starting
- Establish a management system, integrated into the business, to maintain and continually improve the program
- Follow the plan-do-check-act model and refer to the ISO 14001 standard.

Notes

Disclaimer: The statements presented in this chapter are those of the individual authors, based on their personal experience working as practitioners in this field.

References

Distribution Business Management Association. "Circle of Excellence Award," n.d., accessed July 3, 2019, www.dcenter.com/education-awards/awards/circle-of-excellence-award.

EPA Center for Corporate Climate Leadership. "2013 Climate Leadership Award Winners," 2013, https://www.epa.gov/climateleadership/2013-climate-leadership-award-winners#IBM.

IBM. *IBM Supplier Conduct Principles*, November 2004, https://www.ibm.com/procurement/scarchived.wss.

——. 2018 *Corporate Responsibility Report*, 2019: 14–23, https://www.ibm.org/static/responsibility/cr/pdfs/IBM-2018-CRR.pdf.

———. *Environmental Affairs Policy*, n.d.a., accessed July 3, 2019, https://www.ibm.com/ibm/environment/policy/.

———. *Social and Environmental Management System Supplier Requirements*, n.d.b., last accessed July 3, 2019, https://www.ibm.com/procurement/semsSuppReq.wss.

———. *Management Principles & Practices*, n.d.c., accessed July 7, 2021, https://www.ibm.com/ibm/history/documents/pdf/management.pdf.

Responsible Business Alliance. *RBA Code of Conduct 6.0*, n.d., accessed July 3, 2019, www.responsiblebusiness.org/code-of-conduct/.

SDC Executive. "ISM Honors IBM for Global Sustainability & Supply Chain Management," Press Release, June 11, 2011, https://www.sdcexec.com/home/press-release/10309028/ism-honors-ibm-for-global-sustainability-supply-chain-management.

Woody, Todd. "I.B.M. Suppliers Must Track Environmental Data." *The New York Times*, April 14, 2010, https://green.blogs.nytimes.com//2010/04/14/ibm-will-require-suppliers-to-track-environmental-data/.

Chapter 6

Regional deals, international players

Augusta C.F. Wilson

States: the laboratories of climate change solutions?

Despite the scientific consensus that climate change has human causes, in the United States the federal government has yet to implement any overarching policy to address it. Of the numerous other parties, both public and private, that have stepped in to develop solutions in the absence of federal action, one of the most successful and most interesting has been the US states. State-level actors of various kinds have developed new partnerships and innovative ways to reduce greenhouse gas (GHG) emissions and advance climate policy by collaborating with each other.

One of the primary ways in which states have collaborated to reduce GHG emissions is through the formation of regional GHG cap-and-trade markets. Under a cap-and-trade regime, the government decides which facilities or economic sectors will be covered by the program and then sets an emissions cap that represents the total allowed emissions from all covered sources of GHGs. Tradeable emissions allowances, each authorizing the release of a specified amount of GHGs with the total equaling the overall emissions cap, are then distributed to covered sources. At the end of each compliance period, covered entities must submit allowances representing the amount of their actual GHG emissions during the period.

The origins of North American greenhouse gas cap-and-trade markets

The concept of using cap-and-trade markets to reduce emissions has some of its earliest origins in theories developed by the economist Ronald Coase, who argued that legal regimes relying on explicit and transferable property rights would most effectively address negative externalities, because they would create incentives for those property rights to inure to their highest-value use (Tietenberg, 2010). Economists John Dales and Thomas Crocker were among the first to conceptualize how the principle could be applied to develop permit markets that could control air and water pollution (Dickinson,

DOI: 10.4324/9780429281242-7

2010). Of potential policy solutions for addressing climate change, cap-and-trade markets are often favored because they offer a market-based approach to reducing GHG emissions. By setting caps on GHG emissions but then allowing polluters to freely purchase the right to emit, cap-and-trade markets can, in theory, allow the regulated entities to determine the cheapest way to meet the desired emissions targets. Thus, well-executed cap-and-trade markets can offer an efficient approach to reducing GHG emissions.

There was an attempt in Congress in 2010 to institute a federal cap-and-trade program, often referred to as the Waxman–Markey climate and energy bill (Walsh, 2010), but it was unsuccessful. Given the current political climate, it seems unlikely that any federal program instituting cap-and-trade or a carbon tax will be implemented any time soon. However, states have collaborated to develop regional cap-and-trade programs. The United States' first multi-state cap-and-trade program was the Regional Greenhouse Gas Initiative (RGGI), which formally began in 2009 and is a partnership of 11 states in the Northeast and mid-Atlantic. The other, the Western Climate Initiative (WCI), is a partnership between California and the Canadian province of Quebec, which held its first joint auction in 2014. Numerous other jurisdictions have signed on to the WCI and remain observers. California and Quebec, however, are currently the only ones participating in joint auctions. Calls have even been made for the RGGI and WCI to link. In 2006, then-Governors George Pataki of New York and Arnold Schwarzenegger of California announced that they would pursue a partnership between their states (Matthews, 2006).[1] In 2015, New York Governor Andrew Cuomo again announced that New York would engage with its RGGI partners, California, Ontario, and Quebec, to explore the possibility of a formal linkage (Office of Governor Andrew Cuomo).

Arguments for and against cap-and-trade

While the vision of a broad North American carbon market has yet to come to fruition—possibly because of some of the logistical and political challenges with linkage that will be discussed in more detail later in this chapter—commentators generally seem to agree that, if well planned and executed, linking regional carbon markets can offer several important benefits to the participating jurisdictions. These benefits largely derive from the fact that jurisdictions will have different marginal costs of abating carbon pollution, depending on the mix of electricity generation technologies they employ and (to the extent the cap-and-trade program covers sectors of the economy beyond the electricity sector) their specific economies (Dion, 2016). Linking markets allows an equalization of these costs. The jurisdiction with the higher marginal cost of abatement benefits because sources there can purchase allowances from the other jurisdiction at relatively low cost, allowing it to achieve its emissions reduction goals more cheaply than it otherwise could (Ranson and Stavins, 2015; Wright, 2016). Conversely, the jurisdiction with the lower marginal cost of abatement benefits because sources there can now sell their allowances at higher prices, resulting in an inflow of revenue, while implementing emissions reductions at a lower cost than the price of the allowances they sell (Canada's Ecofiscal Commission, 2015; Ranson and Stavins, 2015).

A related, but distinct, economic argument for linking carbon markets is that connecting them can improve market efficiency because it increases market liquidity. When jurisdictions create linked markets, the number of regulated sources participating in the resulting larger market increases. This simple fact of increased participation makes it easier for participants to trade allowances on the market quickly and at desirable prices, lowering transaction costs. This effect can be particularly important if any of the linking markets are relatively small (International Emissions Trading Association, 2007). The greater number of market participants and available portfolio of options for reducing emissions can also reduce price volatility by helping to "buffer carbon markets against uncertainties that affect costs, such as patterns of economic activity and wea-ther" (Ginocchio, 2016: 10). As with improved liquidity, this effect can be par-ticularly important if any of the linking markets are relatively small.

While linkage can offer these economic benefits, it has potential negative effects as well. Perhaps most important, because one of the linking jurisdictions will necessarily have a lower cost of reducing GHG emissions than the other, regulated entities in this jurisdiction will be inclined to buy the (now available post-linkage) relatively cheaper credits and continue to emit, rather than engage in (now relatively more costly) abatement. Although GHG pollution obviously causes a global problem, this kind of "outsourcing" of emissions reductions can nonetheless cause individual jurisdictions to miss out on many of the ancil-lary benefits associated with reducing GHG emissions: in particular, reductions in emissions of air pollutants like NOx (oxides of nitrogen, which are often emitted from regulated sources along with CO_2) and associated improvements in air quality (Flachsland, Marschinski, and Edenhofer, 2011).

Indeed, one recent study published in the journal *PLOS* found that 52 per-cent of regulated facilities in California reported higher annual average in-state GHG emissions—and correlated co-pollutant emissions—in the first two years after California's cap-and-trade program was initiated than before (Cushing et al., 2018).[2] Because regulated facilities tend to be located in disadvantaged neighborhoods, such as Wilmington in south Los Angeles (Guerin, 2017), that have higher proportions of residents of color and higher rates of poverty, those residents disproportionately miss the benefits of cap-and-trade, or even find that pollution gets worse.

These kinds of challenges require additional solutions. For example, ensuring that the cap on emissions is sufficiently low could help ameliorate this challenge; avoiding an initial abundance of inexpensive allowances would leave fewer regulated entities incentivized to purchase allowances and pollute (Calma, 2018). Increased regulation of problematic GHG co-pollutants or specific geo-graphic restrictions on trading are other solutions sometimes suggested to help mitigate such pollution "hot spots" (Farber, 2012: 45). Requiring that regulated entities purchase any pollution offsets in-state, where they can contribute to local green projects or pollution mitigation, could also help (Calma, 2018).

The potential need for these additional measures is probably part of the reason that GHG cap-and-trade programs seem particularly susceptible to the vagaries of the political winds. For instance, New Jersey was one of the original members of the RGGI, but it withdrew when a Republican governor came into office. It is currently expected to rejoin in 2022, now that the governor's mansion is occupied by a Democrat. In July 2020, Virginia became the first Southern state to join the RGGI after Democrats won control of the state legislature in November 2019.[3]

Considerations for linking regional markets

While regional cap-and-trade programs are clearly far from a perfect solution to climate change, they remain at the forefront of current climate policies in the United States, perhaps because they offer immediate practical benefits (notwithstanding any legitimate debates about their merits as substantive policy). Linking with a regional GHG cap-and-trade market can provide relatively immediate administrative benefits to a participating state. Regulators in linked jurisdictions can share knowledge, experience, and best practices with each other (Burtraw et al., 2013). In addition, linkage can create consistency and stability for regulated entities, first because it is more difficult to change a regulatory scheme when doing so requires coordination with other linked jurisdictions (Bodansky et al., 2014), and second because presumably some regulated entities own facilities in multiple adjoining states and benefit from consistent regulations if those states link their markets.

Finally, and perhaps most tangible in the short-term, by creating joint regional carbon markets states demonstrate that, despite inaction (or even, at times, regression) at the federal level on the issue of climate change, there is political will in large swaths of the United States to reduce GHG emissions (Stewart, 2008; Burtraw et al., 2013). The success of the RGGI and WCI programs has arguably built momentum for the creation of a national GHG cap-and-trade program among states yet to join regional markets, and there is even potential for better international cooperation on climate change.

To successfully build these regional carbon markets, participating jurisdictions have had to work closely together to ensure that their programs were sufficiently compatible for the joint markets. For the RGGI and WCI to work, for example, it was necessary for the programs in the participating states and provinces to have similar stringencies, compatible price control mechanisms, and methods for tracking compliance, among other things. In creating the WCI, which spans international borders, the staffs of the California Air Resources Board and its equivalent in Quebec had to consider how to harmonize these elements. Staffs in both jurisdictions worked closely and collaboratively to solve these and a whole series of similar problems to make the linkage function well (Ministère du Développement Durable, 2015).

Some of the disadvantages of regional carbon markets could be resolved if participating states set more stringent emissions caps. Many of the complaints about cap-and-trade—including the challenges of pollution "outsourcing" and "hot spots" discussed above—would be diminished by setting caps low enough to eliminate surpluses of cheap allowances. Simply having more states participating, particularly geographically contiguous states, would also help to ameliorate some of the challenges with regional cap-and-trade markets. The larger the geographic area such a market covers, the more numerous and diverse the sources it covers, allowing the market to function more smoothly and lessening the likelihood of discrepancies in economic makeup leading to significant challenges with issues such as pollution hotspots and outsourcing. If states can make these adjustments, then regional cap-and-trade markets may continue to be an important part of the mix of climate solutions going forward.

Collaborations among state attorneys general

Regional carbon markets are not the only way states have found to work together on climate change. Another high-profile example is collaboration between and among progressive state AGs. In recent years, state AGs have increasingly acted in concert both to push for affirmative steps to reduce GHG emissions and to oppose attempts to roll back rules and regulations intended to address climate change and reduce GHG emissions.

It is not new for state AGs to coordinate with each other; indeed, at least one commentator has argued that state AGs have been acting in concert since as early as the 1970s (Olson, 2017). Collective action by state AGs ratcheted up a significant notch in 1999, when 12 Republican state AGs formed the Republican Attorneys General Association with the explicit mission of "electing Republicans to the Office of State Attorney General" (Republican Attorneys General Association, n.d.). The Democratic Attorneys General Association was formed a few years later in 2002 (Democratic Attorneys General Association, n.d.). According to former Arizona Attorney General Grant Woods, "[u]p until 1999, the attorneys general were very nonpartisan" (Freidman and Schwartz, 2018). In recent decades, however, state AGs have increasingly become partisan warriors, and during the Obama administration Republican AGs teamed up numerous times to sue the federal government in attempts to block environmental regulations or programs (Nolette, 2014; Freidman and Schwartz, 2018). Perhaps most prominently, a large coalition of Republican state AGs sued to prevent the United States Environmental Protection Agency (EPA) from enacting the Obama administration's Clean Power Plan. Republican state AGs also joined forces with corporate interests at unprecedented levels during the Obama administration (Lipton, 2014).

Democratic state AGs appeared to take a page from that playbook during the Trump administration (Freidman and Schwartz, 2018). For example, within hours of President Trump's inauguration a coalition of Democratic AGs went to court in defense of EPA regulations aimed at reducing cross-state air pollution. Climate change was an area of particular focus for state AGs during this time period. In April 2017, more than a dozen state AGs joined forces to oppose the Trump EPA's attempts to hold litigation over the Clean Power Plan, which had already advanced to late stages, in open-ended abeyance.[4] In July 2017, Hector Balderas, the attorney general of New Mexico, and Xavier Becerra, the attorney general of California, sued to block the Department of the Interior from delaying compliance with methane flaring regulations at oil and gas drilling sites on public and tribal lands (State of California Department of Justice, 2017). Balderas and Becerra sued again in September of 2018 when the Trump administration took steps to dismantle the Obama-era methane waste prevention rule.[5] Coalitions of state AGs also filed federal lawsuits aimed at preventing the Trump administration from delaying implementation of fuel efficiency standards and vehicle emissions rules (New York Attorney General's Press Office, 2017).[6]

This concerted action does not appear to have ended with the Trump administration. For example, when, just days before the inauguration of a new President, the Trump EPA published a surprise final rule that would severely curtail the agency's ability to regulate industrial GHG emissions under section 111 of the Clean Air Act, over a dozen state AGs joined forces to not only bring a lawsuit challenging the rule, but also to push the new Biden administration to take action to remove the rule from the books.[7]. In total, as of July 2021, the State Energy & Environmental Impact Center at NYU School of Law had documented over 500 litigations and other regulatory and policy actions taken by state AGs—often acting in pairs or groups—to protect against federal environmental rollbacks and other harmful federal decisions (State Energy & Environmental Impact Center, n.d.).

This approach has met with some measurable success. For example, state AGs mounted an effective opposition to the Trump EPA's attempts to delay or suspend methane regulations, which sent the agency back to the drawing board (Hayes 2018). After the 2020 election, Congress began taking steps to repeal Trump-era rollbacks of methane regulations and restore Obama-era rules.[8] The Trump administration was unable to implement its much weaker proposed plan to replace the Obama-era Clean Power Plan because of lawsuits led by state AGs.

State AGs have worked together not just to use traditional environmental laws to protect against rollbacks of climate rules, but also to advance innovative litigation strategies to advance climate goals. For example, a number of states, including Connecticut, New York, Massachusetts, Minnesota, and Rhode Island have sued ExxonMobil for allegedly having defrauded investors by "downplaying the expected risks of climate change to its business" (Schwartz, 2018).[9]

One of the interesting challenges these parallel litigations have revealed about the state AGs acting in concert on climate change is that each of the state AGs is working with different state laws. Thus, for example, while New York's lawsuit against ExxonMobil (since dismissed) was brought under a state law that focuses on financial fraud, Massachusetts has focused instead on potential violations of consumer protection laws that make it illegal to engage in unfair or deceptive advertising, including failing to disclose known hazards or risks of a product (Kaufman, 2018). Rhode Island, for its part, was actually the first state to directly sue fossil fuel companies for damages associated with climate change in July 2018, but it chose yet another path; its suit was based on a state law that makes polluting public property a public nuisance. So, while some conservative think tanks and special interest groups have been incensed by what they see as a cabal of left-leaning state AGs teaming up in politically motivated attacks (Heartland Institute, 2017), developing novel strategies for protecting and strengthening climate regulations may mean that even where states wish to work together in a coordinated fashion their approaches will ultimately need to diverge, particularly if those strategies involve litigation, since state laws may dictate different approaches.

The necessity for this type of patchwork approach can pose challenges, particularly with respect to a global issue that so clearly seems to call for uniform policy solutions applied throughout the widest possible geographic areas. On the conservative side of the spectrum, the American Legislative Exchange Council (ALEC)—an organization that serves to bring conservative state legislators and business interests together to draft and share model state legislation for distribution to state legislatures all over the country—has been in place for decades to address this type of problem. Perhaps the next phase of this fight will be a push in states where the political will exists to adopt laws that make a more unified strategy feasible. Indeed, Professors Michael Gerrard and John Dernbach's *Legal Pathways to Deep Decarbonization in the United States* (2019), a large compilation of ideas from dozens of lawyers from across the US, offers policies that would dramatically cut GHG pollution. Gerrard and Dernbach are now organizing lawyers to write laws based on these proposals that can be distributed to lawmakers (Deaton 2019).

Collaborating at all levels

State AGs are not the only state-level actors who have been collaborating to act on climate change: governors, too, have begun creating formal organizations and coalitions with the explicit mission of using the power of their offices to act on climate change. On June 1, 2017, when President Trump announced that he would pull the US out of the Paris Climate Agreement, the governors of

New York, California, and Washington issued statements announcing that they were forming a new state coalition called the United States Climate Alliance (Plummer, 2019; Sommerhauser, 2019). They announced that they were committed to "conven[ing] US states committed to upholding the Paris Climate Agreement and taking aggressive action on climate change" in the absence of federal government action on the issue. They also planned to "act as a forum to sustain and strengthen existing climate programs, promote the sharing of information and best practices, and implement new programs to reduce carbon emissions from all sectors of the economy" (Washington Governor's Office, 2017). In the days that followed, other governors—including the Republican governors of Massachusetts and Vermont—announced that they would join the Alliance. As of July 2021, 24 states and Puerto Rico have joined.

The Alliance not only provides the participating states an important platform for developing and publicizing their own regulatory and policy initiatives on climate change, but it also allows the participating states to actively build on each other's best practices and collaborate to develop new joint initiatives: for example, to develop new clean energy finance opportunities. They collaborated on an initiative whereby the New York Green Bank will raise private capital that can be deployed outside New York to stimulate clean energy across Alliance states. Alliance states also announced they are working together and with industry to develop new and updated energy efficiency standards for appliances that will help achieve emissions reduction targets (United States Climate Alliance, n.d.). In September 2018, they also held a widely publicized Global Climate Action Summit in San Francisco.

US cities have also gotten involved and have, in some cases, teamed up to file climate change-related lawsuits. For instance, Oakland and San Francisco filed a case against five of the world's largest fossil fuel companies, seeking to obtain damages for the costs of mitigating and responding to climate change from those companies under a public nuisance theory.[10] The types of common law theories these cases have tended to use, like nuisance or public trust, to the extent they have been used in the environmental context, have more traditionally been applied to fact patterns involving pollutants with strong odors or visible emissions, or the preservation of public parks. So far, courts have not been particularly receptive to cases in which cities have attempted to call upon these doctrines to address damages relating to climate change and most have been dismissed.

The US Climate Alliance, which has focused on policy solutions rather than litigation, has had more success. As of 2016 Alliance states were more than halfway to meeting their share of the goal that the United States committed to in the Paris Agreement, a 26 to 28 percent reduction in GHG emissions to below 2005 levels by 2025 (United States Climate Alliance, 2018a). Moreover, the participating states have pledged to carry out policies that they likely could not achieve independently. For example, in July 2020 Alliance members announced a joint MOU to collaborate on a multi-state action plan to creating a zero-emissions medium- and heavy-duty vehicle market (United States Climate Alliance, 2020).

These kinds of collaborations come with notable challenges, just as cap-and-trade markets do. Even though the state AGs pushing for action on climate change are hardly the first to work together in such a way, it is nonetheless easy for critics to paint the lawsuits and other actions they are taking as coordinated, politically motivated attacks intended to raise the profiles of would-be rising stars in the Democratic Party. The very existence of the State Energy & Environment Impact Center at NYU Law School—which has placed fellows at state AG offices for the explicit purpose of "helping state AGs fight against regulatory rollbacks and advocate for clean energy, climate change, and environmental values and protections"—has infuriated conservative commentators and interest groups (Horner, 2018) and has prompted organizations like the Competitive Enterprise Institute (CEI) to use open records laws to probe what they see as an "interconnected web" of law schools, private funders, law enforcement, and other litigators to benefit what they term the "climate litigation industry." CEI, for example, filed an open records request with the University of California at Los Angeles Law School seeking documents relating to what CEI believes to be some UCLA Law professors' role in working with an effort "led by activist groups and the Attorney General of New York" to "develop theories of litigation against, and pursue as targets of investigation, perceived opponents of a political and policy agenda shared by these outside parties and certain faculty."[11]

Another important challenge faced by these collaborations among states is the global nature of the climate crisis, which means that while regional carbon-trading programs like the RGGI and WCI, and multi-state collaborations like the US Climate Alliance, have been able to take meaningful steps, realistically they cannot be enough in the longer term. The states in the US Climate Alliance represent only about 25 percent of total US greenhouse gas emissions (Fouré and Bellora, 2018). A recent report from Data-Driven Yale found that in the United States full implementation of all the city, regional, and company commitments to greenhouse gas reductions that have been reported and quantified so far could reduce emissions "at least half way" to what would be needed to achieve the United States' Paris pledge (Hsu et al., 2018). These numbers are by no means to be dismissed; they are substantial and clearly illustrate how powerful subnational jurisdictions can be, especially when they act in concert. They are clearly insufficient, however, to address the global climate change problem on their own.

In the long term, collaborations between states to address climate change can only be effective if they succeed in building momentum. The success of multi-state climate initiatives will ultimately be defined by whether they can bring increasing numbers of partners on board, and this will likely need to include international partners. That would demonstrate to the rest of the world that there is the political will in the United States to address climate change and that there are partners here with whom other countries can work.

In this light, it is extremely promising that Mexico and Canada have been involved with US Climate Alliance initiatives, collectively committing to reach 50 percent zero-carbon power generation across North America by 2025 and accepting the US Climate Alliance's short-lived Climate Pollutant Challenge (United States Climate Alliance, 2018b). This is not the only successful international coalition involving US states, either. The Under2 Coalition, formed in 2015, has more than 200 signatories and endorsers in at least 43 countries (Alex, 2018). These signatories include not just states but many US cities, which, as noted above, are becoming increasingly active on climate change, both individually and in coalitions. These are promising signs that these kinds of regional collaborations between states and other sub-federal actors can attract international partners and have more than just a regional influence.

Notes

1 Governor Schwarzenegger also signed an executive order calling for the creation of a program that would allow the WCI to link with the RGGI. *Executive Order No. S-20-06 (2006)*, https://www.gov.ca.gov/news.php?id=4484.

2 It is crucial to clarify that this study was examining the implementation of California's program *before* joint auctions with Quebec began. Thus, the challenges it details are not specifically due to or related to *linking* preexisting carbon markets, but, rather, are problems inherent to cap-and-trade programs in general. However, this still exemplifies the kind of problem that linking can exacerbate.

3 See https://grist.org/beacon/virginia-joins-the-cap-and-trade-club/ .

4 State and Municipal Respondent-Intervenor's Opposition to Motion to Hold Proceeding in Abeyance, *State of West Virginia et al. v. U.S. Environmental Protection Agency et al.*, No. 15-1363 (D.C. Cir.), April 5, 2017, https://ag.ny.gov/sites/default/files/2017_04_05_opposition_to_abeyance_motion_filed.pdf.

5 Complaint for Declaratory and Injunctive Relief, *State of California et al. v. Zinke et al.*, No. 3:18 cv 05712 (N.D. Cal.), September 18, 2018, https://oag.ca.gov/system/files/attachments/press-docs/18-05712-california-v-zinke-complaint.pdf.

6 Petition for Review of Final Agency Action, *State of California et al. v. U.S. Environmental Protection Agency* (D.C. Cir.), https://oag.ca.gov/system/files/attachments/press_releases/2018-05-01%20Petition%20Revised%20MTE.pdf.

7 See https://oag.ca.gov/news/press-releases/attorney-general-becerra-leads-challenge-trump-administration-rule-blocking and https://www.law.nyu.edu/sites/default/files/ags-petition-reconsideration-epa-ghg-significant-contribution-rule.pdf.

8 See https://www.jdsupra.com/legalnews/congress-repeals-trump-era-methane-rule-6088441/ and https://www.coloradopolitics.com/news/congress-votes-to-reinstate-methane-rules-loosened-by-trump/article_1abd5f9e-7cca-56af-9d71-7007e899d596.html.

9 See also https://insideclimatenews.org/news/15092020/climate-change-lawsuit-connecticut-deleware/.

10 Order Granting Motion to Dismiss Amended Complaints, *City of Oakland et al. v BP P.L.C. et al.*, Nos. C 17-06011 and C 17-06012 (N.D. Cal.), June 25, 2018, https://assets.documentcloud.org/documents/4560042/Judge-Alsup-Dismisses-Climate-Suit-Against-Oil.pdf?smid=nytcore-ios-share.

11 Verified Petition for Peremptory Writ of Mandate and Write of Mandate Ordering Compliance with the California Public Records Act, *Competitive Enterprise Institute v. The Regents of the University of California and Does* 1-30, No. 18 ST CP 02832 (Cal. Super. Ct. L.A. Cent. Dist.), November 8, 2018, http://blogs2.law.columbia.edu/climate-change-litigation/wp-content/uploads/sites/16/case-documents/2018/20181108_docket-18-ST-CP-02832_petition-for-writ-of-mandate.pdf.

References

Alex, Ken. "Three Years of the Under2 Coalition," The Climate Group, May 21, 2018, https://www.theclimategroup.org/our-work/states-and-regions-under2-coalition.

Bodansky, Daniel M., Seth A. Hoedl, Gilbert E. Metcalf, and Robert N. Stavins. *Facilitating Linkage of Heterogeneous Regional, National, and Sub-National Climate Policies Through a Future International Agreement, Harvard Project on Climate Agreements,* 2014, https://www.belfercenter.org/sites/default/files/files/publication/harvard-ieta-linkage-paper-nov-2014.pdf.

Burtraw, Dallas, Karen Palmer, Clayton Munnings, Paige Weber, and Matt Woerman. *Linking by Degrees: Incremental Alignment of Cap-and-Trade Markets,* Resources for the Future, Discussion Paper No. 13-04, 2013.

Calma, Justine. "How California Can Make Its Cap-and-Trade Program More Equitable," *Grist,* July 18, 2018, https://grist.org/article/how-california-can-make-its-cap-and-trade-program-more-equitable/.

Canada's Ecofiscal Commission. *The Way Forward: A Practical Approach to Reducing Canada's Greenhouse Gas Emissions,* 2015, http://ecofiscal.ca/wp-content/uploads/2015/04/Ecofiscal-Commission-Report-The-Way-Forward-April-2015.pdf.

Cushing, L., D. Blaustein-Rejto, M. Wander, M. Pastor et al. "Carbon Trading, Co-Pollutants, and Environmental Equity: Evidence from California's Cap-and-Trade Program (2011–2015)," *PLoS Med* 15, no. 7 (2018): e1002604, https://doi.org/10.1371/journal.pmed.1002604.

Deaton, Jeremy. "These Lawyers are Creating an ALEC for Climate Change," *Nexus News,* April 1, 2019, https://nexusmedianews.com/these-lawyers-are-creating-an-alec-for-climate-change-67cbd081e828/.

Democratic Attorneys General Association, n.d., accessed July 9, 2021, https://dems.ag/.

Dickinson, Elizabeth. "Capping it Off: How a Concept Became an Environmental Policy Catchphrase," *Foreign Policy,* February 19, 2010, https://foreignpolicy.com/2010/02/19/capping-it-off/.

Dion, Jason. *Unpacking the WCI: Thinking Linking,* Canada's Ecofiscal Commission, June 29, 2016, https://ecofiscal.ca/2016/06/29/unpacking-wci-thinking-linking/.

Farber, Daniel A. "Pollution Markets and Social Equity: Analyzing the Fairness of Cap and Trade," *Ecology Law Quarterly* 39, No. 1 (2012): 1–56.

Flachsland, Christian, Robert Marschinski, and Ottmar Edenhofer. "To Link or Not to Link: Benefits and Disadvantages of Linking Cap-and-Trade Systems," *Climate Policy* 9 (2011): 361–2.

Fouré, Jean and Cecilla Bellora. "U.S. Withdrawal from the Paris Agreement: Can States Lead the Fight to Reduce Carbon Emissions?" *The Conversation*, January 28, 2018, http://theconversation.com/us-withdrawal-from-the-paris-agreement-can-states-lead-the-fight-to-reduce-carbon-emissions-89882.

Freidman, Lisa and John Schwartz. "Borrowing G.O.P. Playbook, Democratic States Sue the Government and Rack Up Wins," *The New York Times*, March 21, 2018, https://www.nytimes.com/2018/03/21/climate/attorneys-general-trump-environment-lawsuits.html.

Gerrard, Michael and John Dernbach. *Legal Pathways to Deep Decarbonization in the United States*. Washington, DC: Environmental Law Institute, 2019.

Ginocchio, Alaine. *Linking to Obtain the Potential Benefits of Broader Carbon Markets: Considerations for Western States*. Western Interstate Energy Board, 2016, https://www.westernenergyboard.org/wp-content/uploads/2017/03/10-14-16-DRAFT-sep-linkage-benefits-considerations-for-western-states-brief-1.pdf.

Guerin, Emily. "Environmental Groups Say California's Climate Program Has Not Helped Them," National Public Radio, February 24, 2017, https://www.npr.org/2017/02/24/515379885/environmental-groups-say-californias-climate-program-has-not-helped-them.

Hasemyer, David. "Fossil Fuels on Trial: Where the Major Climate Change Law Suits Stand Today," *Inside Climate News*, January 6, 2019, https://insideclimatenews.org/news/04042018/climate-change-fossil-fuel-company-lawsuits-timeline-exxon-children-california-cities-attorney-general.

Hayes, David J. "Trump's Biggest Attempts to Roll Back Environmental Regulations Remain at the Starting Gate," *Slate*, October 22, 2018, https://slate.com/technology/2018/10/trump-methane-emissions-deregulation-is-failing.html.

Heartland Institute. "State Attorneys General Launch Legal Attack on Climate Realists," March 28, 2017, https://www.heartland.org/topics/climate-change/state-attorneys-general-launch-legal-attack-climate-realists/index.html.

Horner, Christopher C. "Law Enforcement for Rent: How Special Interests Fund Climate Policy Through State Attorneys General," Competitive Enterprise Institute, August 28, 2018, https://cei.org/AGclimatescheme.

Hsu, Angel et al. *Global Climate Action from Cities, Regions, and Businesses*, Data Driven Yale, NewClimate Institute, PBL Netherlands Environmental Assessment Agency, 2018, https://datadrivenlab.org/wp-content/uploads/2018/08/YALE-NCI-PBL_Global_climate_action.pdf.

International Emissions Trading Association. *IETA Report on Linking GHG Emissions Trading Systems*, 2007, https://pdfs.semanticscholar.org/491c/a80e6306a411ef566dd6c278b5a081e17437.pdf.

Kaufman, Alexander C. "Wins by Democratic Attorneys General Threaten to Multiply Climate Suits Against Big Oil," *Huffington Post*, November 10, 2018, https://www.huffingtonpost.com/entry/midterms-democrats-attorney-general-climate-lawsuits_us_5be5f199e4b0e8438897aa58.

Lipton, Eric. "Energy Firms in Secretive Alliance with Attorneys General," *The New York Times*, December 6, 2014, https://www.nytimes.com/2014/12/07/us/politics/energy-firms-in-secretive-alliance-with-attorneys-general.html.

Matthews, Karen. "Schwarzenegger Pushes Emission Markets," *The Washington Post*, October 17, 2006, www.washingtonpost.com/wp-dyn/content/article/2006/10/16/AR2006101600165.html.

Ministère du Développement Durable, de l'Environnement et de la Lutte contre les Changements Climatiques, Gouvernement du Quebec. "Quebec Cap-and-Trade System: Pioneering the Linking of a Regional Carbon Market," in *Emissions Trading Worldwide, International Carbon Action Partnership Status Report 2015*, https://icapcarbonaction.com/en/status-report-2015.

New York Attorney General's Press Office. "A.G. Schneiderman Leads New Lawsuit to Protect Fuel Efficiency Standards," Press Release, September 11, 2017, https://ag.ny.gov/press-release/ag-schneiderman-leads-new-lawsuit-protect-fuel-efficiency-standards.

Nolette, Paul. "State Litigation During the Obama Administration: Diverging Agendas in an Era of Polarized Politics," *Publius*, Summer 2014, https://epublications.marquette.edu/cgi/viewcontent.cgi?referer=https://www.google.com/&httpsredir=1&article=1013&context=polisci_fac.

Office of Governor Andrew Cuomo. "Governor Cuomo Announces New Actions to Reduce Greenhouse Gas Emissions and Lead Nation on Climate Change," Press Release, October 8, 2015, https://www.governor.ny.gov/news/governor-cuomo-joined-vice-president-gore-announces-new-actions-reduce-greenhouse-gas-emissions.

Olson, Walter. "Partisan Prosecutions: How State Attorneys General Dove into Politics," *New York Post*, March 30, 2017, https://nypost.com/2017/03/30/partisan-prosecutions-how-state-attorneys-general-dove-into-politics/.

Ranson, Matthew and Robert N. Stavins. "Linkage of Greenhouse Gas Emissions Trading Systems: Learning from Experience," *Climate Policy* 16 (2015): 284–300.

Republican Attorneys General Association. "About RAGA," n.d., accessed July 2, 2019, https://www.republicanags.com/about/.

Schneider, Gregory S. "Virginia Regulators Vote to Limit Carbon Emissions but Face GOP Roadblock," *The Washington Post*, April 19, 2019, https://www.washingtonpost.com/local/virginia-politics/virginia-regulators-vote-to-limit-carbon-emissions-but-face-gop-roadblock/2019/04/19/0bcc0a18-62db-11e9-9412-daf3d2e67c6d_story.html?utm_term=.490797c7b46f.

Schwartz, John. "New York Sues Exxon Mobil, Saying it Deceived Shareholders on Climate Change," *The New York Times*, October 24, 2018, https://www.nytimes.com/2018/10/24/climate/exxon-lawsuit-climate-change.html.

Sommerhauser, Mark. "Wisconsin Governor Joins Climate Alliance Committed to Cutting Greenhouse Gases," *Governing*, February 14, 2019, www.governing.com/topics/transportation-infrastructure/tns-wisconsin-climate-alliance-governors.html.

State Energy & Environmental Impact Center, NYU School of Law. "Lawsuits", n.d. accessed July 2, 2019, https://stateimpactcenter.org/ag-actions.

State of California Department of Justice. "New Lawsuit Filed Today Fights Department of the Interior Delay of Rule Aimed at Limiting Methane Waste," Press Release, July 5, 2017, https://oag.ca.gov/news/press-releases/attorney-general-becerra-trump-administration-illegally-ignores-rule-protects.

Stewart, Richard B. "States and Cities as Actors in Global Climate Change Regulation: Unitary vs. Plural Architectures," *Arizona Law Review* 50, no. 3 (2008): 681–707.

Tietenberg, T. "Cap and Trade: The Evolution of an Economic Idea," *Agricultural and Economics Review* 359 (October 2010): 360–1, https://ageconsearch.umn.edu/bitstream/95836/2/tietenberg%20-%20current.pdf.

United States Climate Alliance. "About the Initiatives," n.d., accessed July 2, 2019, www.usclimatealliance.org/efficiency-challenge.

———. *Fighting for Our Future, United States Climate Alliance 2018 Annual Report*, 2018a, https://static1.squarespace.com/static/5a4cfbfe18b27d4da21c9361/t/5b9bda1d1ae6cf830c7f80a7/1536940617096/USCA_2018+Annual+Report_20180911-FINAL.pdf.

———. "Joint Statement on North American Climate Leadership," September 13, 2018b, https://www.usclimatealliance.org/international-cooperation/.

———. *Leading the Charge, United States Climate Alliance 2020 Annual Report*, 2020, https://static1.squarespace.com/static/5a4cfbfe18b27d4da21c9361/t/5f6cacb1258a2d77dedbf60c/1600957656553/USCA_2020+Annual+Report_Leading+the+Charge.pdf.

Walsh, Bryan. "Why the Climate Bill Died," *Time*, July 26, 2010, http://science.time.com/2010/07/26/why-the-climate-bill-died/.

Washington Governor's Office. "Inslee, New York Governor Cuomo, and California Governor Brown Announce Formation of United States Climate Alliance," Press Release, June 1, 2017, https://www.governor.wa.gov/news-media/inslee-new-york-governor-cuomo-and-california-governor-brown-announce-formation-united.

Wright, David V. "Cross-Border Constraints on Climate Change Agreements: Legal Risks in the California-Québec Cap-and-Trade Linkage," *Environmental Law Reporter* 46 (2016): 10478–95.

Conclusion

A growing number of US states, local governments, and leaders in the private sector are poised to build their own deep strategic responses to climate change and the threats it poses to residents and businesses. These forces are pulling themselves toward achieving a state of climate resilience that does not depend on mercurial federal leadership, but on their own resources and with those public and private actors who are aligned with their goals.

As momentum builds toward reaching the goal of climate resilience, the efforts outlined in this volume provide guidance across a wide variety of situations and locations, and show that collaborative efforts on behalf of climate resilience can indeed succeed.

Across widely different circumstances, locations, and actors, key themes and strategies for success stand out. These themes and strategies emerge consistently.

Uncover impacts of concern, find common values, and anchor efforts around them

Groups that initially appeared to have varying perspectives on more abstract concepts of climate change nonetheless found they came to agree on likely impacts and shared common values that inspired them to tackle what lay ahead. Discovering these shared values led team members to trust each other's motivations and to think outside their usual isolated frameworks, inventing a new way of approaching their challenges.

Sometimes the common values were anchored in similar laws and a shared view of justice. This was the case with the state AGs who joined together in joint litigation efforts. Common values surfaced in some cases with the abandonment of politically charged terms such as climate change. The RAFT project in coastal Virginia exemplified this principle, finding they didn't need to talk about whether climate change was real or not. Instead, all found common perspectives regarding possible local impacts on people living in the area. Everyone could agree that survival was a shared value and that local economies and communities would likely continue to be threatened by storms and flooding.

DOI: 10.4324/9780429281242-8

Similarly, Detroiters Working for Environmental Justice (DWEJ), working with 26 stakeholders from many sectors of the city, with analytical support from academic partners, zeroed in on identifying Detroit's specific local vulnerabilities. The group then took the draft frameworks into Detroit communities to identify and test the action steps to address vulnerabilities. This verified the path ahead in ways that empowered and relied on communities. The approach led to the Detroit Smart Neighborhood job-training program and the Climate Ambassador program, which gathered neighborhood residents to install rain barrels and gardens to combat flooding.

Avoid slogans in favor of achieving constructive results

Successful efforts avoided the use of punitive or critical language toward other participants and their beliefs. This is notable mainly because issues surrounding climate are often marked by vitriolic language on all sides. Avoiding acrimony created a dynamic of mutual respect and safety, which ultimately led to trust, creating closer bonds, which then enabled participants to unite behind a common purpose and find approaches all could accept and advocate. For example, Detroit's Sustainability Toolkit helped local businesses improve their energy efficiency in a constructive, supportive way. Coastal Virginia's resilience scorecard, action checklist, and technical support RAFT process also created a system that emphasized measurable results over scoring rhetorical points.

Cast a wide net to include those with knowledge, regardless of their titles or affiliations

In New York, when OneNYC was in its early stages, senior agency leaders were tapped and asked to think beyond their formal duties to identify what could fall within the scope of the new long-term sustainability plan. Forming interdisciplinary and interagency work groups with broad knowledge and jurisdictions led to rich discussions, a more complete picture of the challenges across a wide spectrum, and surprising areas of consensus and creativity. The same dynamic was at play when the US Navy formed its Task Force on Climate Change. In that case, the Navy included a wide range of other agencies and expertise, including NOAA, the US Geological Service, NASA, several national labs, the Interior Department, and even Arctic nations and those with interests in the Artic, such as the United Kingdom, Canada, Norway, Finland, Sweden, Denmark, and Russia. This comprehensive approach is better able to draw in vital facts and expertise, which no one individual, organization, or office can accomplish alone. A diversity of perspectives can raise questions and spot issues that lead to better results.

Embrace flexibility to find the means to an end, including economic tools and other incentives beyond regulation

When a group of states in the Northeast wanted to drive down carbon emissions, they turned to a system that would price those emissions and allow them to be traded. The RGGI's impact came from the motivations that the states set up within this incentivized structure to allow participants to gain benefits from the system. However, those states did not stop with the Northeast; they sought even more flexibility and opportunities when they began talks with the western states and Canadian provinces. While some difficulties emerged, their flexibility opened new areas for collaboration and possible results. Similarly, IBM worked with its suppliers to embed climate and sustainability values into the chain of production. Through the use of agreements and principles that drove behavior, IBM could move the market as a leader and then work with its peers to demonstrate how this approach was not only the right thing to do, but also made good business sense. In both cases, the results rippled far beyond the original actors and became part of doing business. For the Hampton Roads region of Virginia, cost-sharing among local, state, and federal governments provides the beginnings of a shared infrastructure focused on addressing flooding and other climate impacts on military installations as well as local communities.

Require data

When identifying the elements of the challenges facing them, the actors in the cases in this book sought data at multiple stages in their efforts. West Point seeks to provide its cadets with the skills to evaluate and assess data for the long term. In other cases, teams often first reached out to other stakeholders and experts to help them better understand the scope of the issues and the potential impacts they were dealing with. For example, the US Navy, as well as The RAFT project teams, studied the situations at hand and explored likely scenarios. Data came from sources such as NASA and NOAA in the case of the Navy, as well as regional sources in coastal Virginia, in the case of The RAFT. Other participants vetted the data and added their own to the developing set. In New York City, city agencies charged with keeping statistics and other government statistical sources provided the initial set. A range of stakeholders and agency experts reviewed draft analyses, revised them, and submitted them for further review. In the case of the RGGI, data on greenhouse gas emissions and an agreed-upon accounting protocol underpinned the regional effort.

Data in these cases includes qualitative as well as quantitative data. Statistics collected by agencies and others are critical, but not the entire picture. DWEJ used information from stakeholders who could speak to local conditions but had not necessarily kept statistics on them. IBM sought information from signatories and others to assess progress, set new goals, and improve performance in future rounds. Independent audits assessed compliance, increasing transparency and, hence, confidence in the results.

Data serves several important functions in collaborative efforts for climate resilience. First, without defining a problem accurately, it is virtually impossible to devise a solution or strategy. If the data is incomplete, skewed, or inaccurate, any policy or other effort is bound to fail, as it will be solving the wrong problem. In addition, the root causes may be missed.

Second, cooperative acts of defining the data needed, collecting it, and then reviewing it serve to unify the project participants and team members. The process becomes a way to promote alliances and cohesion, find agreement, and reinforce or refine shared values.

Third, having data from the start of the process is key to establishing a baseline for measuring progress and the effectiveness of the adopted plans and initiatives. During program implementation, data show where a program or initiative could be improved and whether the initial approaches do in fact lead to the projected results. If they do not, the program can be modified and improved, thus instituting a process of continuous improvement more likely to lead to real, long-term results that can pave the way to further collaborations.

Take the long view, but include deadlines and accountability to keep the program on track

Achieving resilience in the face of climate impacts requires taking a long view and putting in place stable structures—administrative as well as physical—that may not exist initially. This takes time and investment. For such initiatives to succeed, interim targets and accountability procedures are vital. Requiring transparency on progress can also promote accountability and serves to strengthen a program's integrity. Moreover, instituting deadlines and accountability should be closely tied to data and values. Data that demonstrate progress—or the lack thereof—serve to reinforce the push toward common goals. In fact, if the data do not show progress, shared values can spur teams to adjust, ensuring that the programs stay on track.

The RGGI and its counterparts in other parts of North America instituted a review and evaluation mechanism that has served its members well for the past 20 years. OneNYC—like PlaNYC established before it—announced long-term goals that the city would strive to achieve using interim annual reports, metrics, and indicators to keep track. IBM's system of independent auditors provides yet another level of accountability, with a third party evaluating results. The RAFT initiative embeds evaluation and metrics into its three-part system, with outside expertise providing support to the participants.

Continue to improve, take stock, and look to the future

Collaborating to achieve resilience in the face of climate change lasts beyond any initial announcement. It must look to the future. Collaboration extends to implementation, and at its best is a commitment to getting the answers right for the long term. This means taking data on indicators, metrics, and targets; evaluating progress beginning with the adopted strategies; and reengineering them in light of experience.

This approach is by nature flexible and responsive, accounting for changing conditions, institutions, and goals. It is a circular approach: a spiral that picks up information and adjusts itself along the way. At one stage, it may resemble the DoD efforts in Tidewater Virginia, in conjunction with neighboring jurisdictions, which pool information, strategies, and resources. At another stage, it may resemble the mature RGGI process in the Northeast, which has refined its initial strategy over the last 20 years to take account of the most recent data, methods, and thinking on incentives and markets. IBM provides yet another instance, where the company, its partners, and suppliers have collaborated for many years to advance sustainable operations, but reconvene regularly to take stock and push their targets higher.

Put aside fear and turf

The road necessary for global action on climate resilience travels through the local, state, and regional levels. It is at these levels that the impacts are already being felt, and where people are most motivated to prepare and take action for the sake of their own families, businesses, and communities. Many decisions on energy, waterfronts, ecosystems, and local economies are made near to home. Local residents and institutions are taking action themselves rather than waiting for outside forces to save them. These efforts are empowering, creative, and brave. Rooted in facts and common values, they are grounded in consensus. They have formed new structures and ways of interacting that affirm and strengthen a range of sectors, and include those who have not necessarily had a seat at the table in the past or through national efforts. They are nimble and democratic.

Efforts such as these provide models of how to achieve resilience for those communities that will—and are—already bearing the burdens of climate change.

In other words, all of us.

Index

Printed in the United States
by Baker & Taylor Publisher Services